YOUR LIFE HAS MEANING

DISCOVERING YOUR ROLE in an EPIC STORY

LUKE GEORGE THOMPSON

NORTHWESTERN PUBLISHING HOUSE
Milwaukee, Wisconsin

Northwestern Publishing House
N16W23379 Stone Ridge Dr., Waukesha, WI 53188-1108
www.nph.net
© 2019 Northwestern Publishing House
Published 2019
Printed in the United States of America
ISBN 978-0-8100-3079-4
ISBN 978-0-8100-3080-0 (e-book)

21 22 23 24 25 26 27 28 29 30   11 10 9 8 7 6 5 4 3 2

CONTENTS

I started writing this book some ten years ago while teaching philosophy and logic at a college in the United States. It was then that I first discussed "Broken Chair" with my students. And ten years later, I'm still having discussions about that song with young adults. I'm indebted to these many students, both the students at the institutions where I taught and the students I now minister to as a campus pastor in Ottawa, ON.

But this book really began nearly 20 years ago in Dr. Greg Schulz' philosophy classes. He introduced me to many of the thoughts in this volume, such as Sartre's dialogue with Augustine, Sisyphus' rock, and Nietzsche's madman. He encouraged me to pursue graduate studies in philosophy. He also helped me find Christ among the philosophers. From the seeds he planted so long ago, he'll find much has grown.

Luke George Thompson

"Droll thing, life is—that mysterious arrangement of merciless logic for a futile purpose. The most you can hope from it is some knowledge of yourself—that comes too late—a crop of unextinguishable regrets. I have wrestled with death. It is the most unexciting contest you can imagine. It takes place in an impalpable greyness, with nothing underfoot, with nothing around, without spectators, without clamour, without glory, without the great desire of victory, without the great fear of defeat, in a sickly atmosphere of tepid skepticism, without much belief in your own right, and still less in that of your adversary. If such is the form of ultimate wisdom, then life is a greater riddle than some of us think it to be. I was within a hair's breadth of the last opportunity for pronouncement, and I found with humiliation that probably I would have nothing to say."

Joseph Conrad, *Heart of Darkness*

"There, peeping among the cloud-wrack above a dark [tower] high up in the mountains, Sam saw a white star twinkle for a while. The beauty of it smote his heart, as he looked up out of the forsaken land, and hope returned to him. For like a shaft, clear and cold, the thought pierced him that in the end the Shadow was only a small and passing thing: there was light and high beauty for ever beyond its reach."

J. R. R. Tolkien, *The Return of the King*

"I am writing you a new command; its truth is seen in him and in you, because the darkness is passing and the true light is already shining."

1 John 2:8

one

EVERYTHING IS
MEANINGLESS

———•———

"That's my life. Nothing stays together; things are just, well, falling apart." A hush fell over the room as it started to sink in.

Then another student said, "I think the point is that all of our lives are somehow falling apart. That's how life is."

My Philosophy 101 class members and I had been watching a commercial together. A daughter away at university was using Google Hangouts with her father, who was a clear supporter and source of meaning and purpose in the life of this young woman. The commercial did its job. The viewer definitely wanted to begin using the product to stay connected to what really matters in life: people, relationships, bonds of support and strength. The commercial had a song playing in the background—absolutely gorgeous, velvet music—with the tones and texture of an indie-folk ballad. It was the perfect choice to support the commercial's message of the importance of relationships. When the commercial had finished, the class emanated a gentle, "Aww. . . . "—the reaction you have when you've just watched something beautiful that chokes you up a little. Almost every class for which I played this commercial had this reaction.

"Have you ever noticed that pop music today at times involves an interesting inversion between the sound and the lyrical content?" I asked. "The music expressed the perfect positive vibes the commercial needed to make you emotionally engaged, feeling like something epic and important and meaningful—something with a transcendent eternal quality—is taking place between the daughter and father. But here are the lyrics to the song."

And I put the lyrics up on a slide:

> You breathe, you learn, you lose.
> You take, you break, you choose.
> And as you laugh and cry,
> You do your best and try.
>
> And as the days go by,
> It makes you wonder why
> You try so hard, so hard
> To mend what's bound to fall apart.
>
> Maybe it's time to let it go.
> Maybe it's time for taking it slow.
> Maybe it's time, time, time for anything at all,
> Time, time, time, to let it all fall
> Where it may.

And we talked about how the song by Chris and Thomas is brilliantly titled "Broken Chair"[1] and how it describes life as something polar opposite to what the commercial was using the song's musical vibe to promote. Whereas the commercial's visuals and music worked together to build a sense of dependence on relationships, the lyrics describe a world in which relationships rarely last and probably shouldn't be depended on. Whereas the visuals and music painted a world where everything would be okay, the lyrics disclose a world where everything is "bound to fall apart" and so "it makes you wonder why you try so hard." Whereas the dad-daughter dialogue and the mellow guitar strumming expressed a world in which stability could be achieved (especially with the help of communications software), the lyrics describe life as a broken chair: you can kind of sit in it, but it's uncomfortable and you're afraid of tipping at any moment; there's a constant reminder something is off; the experience is never truly satisfying (regardless of the communications software we've developed!).

And so we find in our culture a conflicting message: on the one hand a voice telling us things can be stable and meaningful, and on the other hand a voice telling us things will never be stable or enduringly meaningful. And often the two voices come from the same mouth.

Which is true? Can stability and contentment be achieved? Is everything fleeting, and so meaning and purpose in life are fleeting? Or is there some way to find and to talk about meaning that lasts?

I didn't even need to ask my class about this conflicting message. As soon as it dawned on them what the song was about, one hand went up: "That's my life."

And then another: "I think the point is that it's all of our lives."

And then murmurs of approval.

And not only with this class. *Every* class that I discussed this song with reached the same conclusion. Life is like sitting on a broken chair.

Music has the ability to do that, to draw out profound truths. But it is not only music that does this. Which is true: is everything fleeting, or is there something with lasting meaning we can be a part of? We might be tempted to think that there's no way to answer this question, that people have been asking and not finding answers to this question for millennia and will continue to do so for many more millennia. But what if three thousand years ago the question was already answered and it was answered in a way that continues to flip our world upside down today, that continues to charge our lives with epic purpose and beauty, that continues to give meaning and purpose—transcending culture, trends, and current philosophies? Even though the smaller stories in our lives contain people who will leave, things that are bound to fall apart, and moments that feel off-kilter, awkward, and unsatisfying, is it possible there is a larger story that we are all a part of, a transcendent plot that promises to make sense of what we experience now, which seems meaningless? What if this larger story can make sense of most of what we experience today and promises to one day answer in full what still baffles us?

Almost three thousand years ago, a Middle Eastern philosopher sat down to write. He spread out his sheet of parchment, and in the first column his pen scratched out these words:

> **"Meaningless! Meaningless!" says the Teacher. "Utterly meaningless! Everything is meaningless." What do people gain from all their labors at which they toil under the sun?**[2]

For this philosopher, there is no time for subtlety. He starts off speaking to us brutally, but honestly. The Teacher (we'll talk about who this Teacher is in a bit) tells us that "under the sun" everything is meaningless.

How could this be true?

Our friends and family members, regardless of their religions or philosophies of life, certainly seem to have meaningful lives. And they'll tell you if you ask them. Ask the father hugging his 5-year-old son if there's no meaning in life. Ask the humanitarian dedicating her life to feeding the poor if there's no meaning in life. Ask the Olympian crossing the finish line if there's no meaning in life. Ask the atheist professor if he finds no value in his work, the agnostic fine artist if she finds no purpose in her paintings, or the Zen Buddhist if he finds no end worth striving for in his dedication to the aesthetic pursuit of gardening, calligraphy, and balance. All will tell you they find deep meaning in what they do. And they're right! To a point.

The first thing we need to do to understand the words of the Teacher correctly, to understand what he *is* and *is not* claiming about life, is to define our terms. What do we *mean* when we say life can or cannot have meaning? And is this what other people mean when they say they have meaningful lives?

The word *meaning* typically has to do with *purpose*. As you sit in class, a person bursts into the room, disturbing everyone, especially your professor, who responds, "What's the meaning of this?" The professor is looking for the *purpose* behind the disruption to her class. The word *meaning* also has to do with *signification,* that is, defining things. Your professor uses a word you don't understand, and you respond, "What's the meaning of that word?" So when we ask, "What's the meaning of life?" we're asking if life has a *purpose* or if we can *define* it. And there are three ways we often talk about life being meaningful in this sense. Let's briefly sketch out each way.

SHORT-TERM MEANING

We can describe life as having *short-term* (or *temporal*) meaning. As autonomous humans, we can choose for certain things to be meaningful and to have value for as long as we value them. Before we valued it, it had no value, and when no one is around to value it, it will no longer be valuable. As an example, consider this news article I came across long ago:

> NEW YORK (Reuters)—Bidders paid top dollar for *Star Trek* items on Thursday at the start of Christie's auction of memorabilia from the television and movie franchise. A model of the Starship *Enterprise E* was bought by an online bidder for $132,000 including commission, more than 10 times its $8,000 to $12,000 presale estimate. The buyer said he had the leftover cash from 35 years of not dating.

We can talk about that spaceship model having meaning because someone found it meaningful, meaningful enough to spend $132,000 dollars on it. It's as simple as that. If people value something, that thing is valuable, and so it has meaning to those people. But consider the reverse: If there hadn't been someone willing to spend *anything* on that spaceship model, it wouldn't have been worth anything. The value of the spaceship is entirely contingent on a person valuing it. The minute something is no longer valued by others—or the thing breaks down, disintegrates, and over time ceases to exist—the value and meaning once associated with the object cease to exist as well.

And this applies to far more than just collectibles. This is typically the kind of "meaning" we have in mind when we talk about our work and our labor in general being meaningful. If you find your own work meaningful, it's because you value it for some reason or another. The most famous physicist of our time, Stephen Hawking, is attributed as saying, "Work gives you meaning and purpose, and life is empty without it." Motivational speaker Les Brown says, "Life takes on meaning when you become motivated, set goals, and charge after them in an unstoppable manner." But ultimately, if a person sets goals in life, to whom are those goals most meaningful? It's possible that they're only meaningful for the person who set them, and that person alone. Maybe striving for or achieving the goals ends up creating something worthwhile for others, and so the value of those goals spills into the lives of others. But once the person who set the goal and the people whom the goal benefited have died, the goal will ultimately cease to have *meaning*. After all, there's no one left to think about it and give it meaning!

For a trivial but interesting example, consider this following story from a newspaper article on bucket lists (each person's personal list of goals to meet in his or her lifetime):

> **Recently, a 99-year-old woman, identified as Annie, decided that she could not die without experiencing being locked up in prison. With the help of her niece and local police, Annie was picked up from her home, placed in a police car, and taken to prison. "We don't usually do this, but we made an**

exception for Annie. It was just a couple of minutes in the cell. It was all about the experience. We don't know why it was on her bucket list," said a police spokesperson.[3]

Annie's family and friends helped her knock an interesting goal off her bucket list: being arrested. The article also included photos of Annie beaming with joy as she was handcuffed and processed at the police station. This was clearly a deeply meaningful experience for her. (And judging from the photos, it left quite an impression on the police officers too.) But as touching and humorous an event as this might have been, over time the meaningfulness of the event will diminish as it fades from the memories of those involved or as they pass away along with their memories. That's why we call this *short-term,* or *temporal,* meaning. It'll exist only for a time. (Philosophers call it "short" because this meaning will be relatively shorter in comparison to the length of time of this universe, whatever that length of time may be.)

The Teacher is talking exactly about this kind of meaning: "What do people gain from all their labors at which they toil under the sun?" Obviously people gain *something* for *some* period of time. But that won't last. "No one remembers the former generations."[4] A time will come when the work of our labors will be forgotten. And when it is forgotten, when it has run its course, it will become *meaningless,* that is, it will lose meaning.

And this doesn't just apply to things or labors or goal-setting but also to relationships. The actor Rebecca Romijn says, "Being a mom makes me feel whole and like I understand the meaning of life." The 20th-century monk Thomas Merton says, "Love is our true destiny. We do not find the meaning of life by ourselves alone—we find it with another." In the song "Meaning Again,"[5] country singer Brad Paisley sings:

Sittin' on the interstate,
The end of another day—
Feeling tired, feeling beat up, feeling small.

> Sick of running this rat race
> And coming last place,
> Feeling like I don't matter at all.
>
> Then I walk through the door.
> She says, "I missed you, where ya been?"
> And just like that
> My life has meaning again.

I remember, like it was yesterday, arguing with a close friend of mine, an atheist, who was saying, "I *do* have meaning in life! I have a partner, kids, friends!" And he was right: When we say human life is *valuable,* we're saying it ought to be valued. And so life *is* meaningful when people value one another. And so life *is* meaningful for the mother and father who now infuse the lives of their children with value. But what my friend didn't want to hear was that a time will come when the mother and father stop valuing their children, if only at death. And the meaning they derived from their lives of valuing their children will die with them.

That's short-term meaning. And, often enough, this is what we mean when we say our life has meaning. We have created relationships with things, jobs, and other people that make us get up in the morning, make us have purpose and goals to strive for, and make our lives *feel* meaningful. But this is short-term. It's there only so long as the person infusing meaning into the situation is there and only so long as that person (or another) is actively valuing.

IS IT ALRIGHT TO STRIVE FOR SHORT-TERM MEANING?

My friend's indignation is a natural reaction. For many of us, we immediately protest against the Teacher, "Life isn't meaningless!" And we're not talking about short-term meaning. We want more than that. We believe human life and happiness have intrinsic value *apart* from however people happen to feel. Yet, some of us might respond to the Teacher, "Well, what's wrong with short-term meaning? Am I doing something *wrong* pursing things because I happen to value them?" Let's ask these questions for a moment. If you think that you *should* be finding short-term meaning in life, the Teacher actually agrees with you.

In the midst of his descriptions of life "under the sun," the Teacher implores us to find satisfaction in our work. He says, "There is nothing better for a person than to enjoy their work, because that is their lot." "It is appropriate for a person to eat, to drink and to find satisfaction in their toilsome labor under the sun." He even starts to sound like that impassioned friend of yours who's telling you to leave that tiresome job and chase your dreams of being a musician or artist or interior decorator: "You who are young, be happy while you are young. . . . Follow the ways of your heart." In other words, it's a great thing in and of itself to find value and meaning and pleasure in something because *you* value it and *you* find meaning in it and *you* enjoy it.

There's a certain feeling, a euphoria, that goes along with accomplishment. It feels *good* to get something done. In 2018, the Philadelphia Eagles won their first Super Bowl. During the presentation of the trophy, the team's owner was asked, "What's this moment mean for the city of Philadelphia?" And he responded, "If there's a word, it's *everything.*" You might be saying, "Everything? Really?" Obviously a city is more than the performance of its sports teams. A trophy, even a Super Bowl trophy, probably doesn't mean *everything,* but we can say it means *something.* It represents countless hours of hard work. It represents a high level of athletic excellence. It represents immense sacrifice for a single goal. Winning that trophy is clearly *meaningful,* not only for the players but for the many fans of the team. And that's a good part of life, says the Teacher: enjoying the accomplishments of hard work and finding satisfaction.

And we're not even talking just about accomplishments. This goes for *anything* out of which we can derive short-term pleasure and value—from *Star Trek* memorabilia collections to relationships, from feeling the world whizz by you on that new motorcycle to stopping to smell the roses, from packed concerts to that quiet walk with your heart's desire. These are all definitely *meaningful* experiences, and there's something to be said for that—even if an experience is *only* meaningful *to you*.

So go ahead! Find short-term meaning in everything you can. After all, this goes for not only sports trophies but graduations, closing business deals, getting to the top of that mountain, finishing that Tough Mudder, getting all *A*s on your report card, watching your daughter walk down the aisle—you name it. Take pleasure in the enjoyment and meaning, because it *is* meaningful.

But what if I want these things in life to be more than simply meaningful *to me*? How can I demonstrate that the people I love ought be loved whether or not *I* love them? Is it possible for things to have meaning and value that transcend personal desires and opinions? And to these questions we turn next.

MORAL MEANING

As I was drinking a cup of tea with my wife, I noticed that the Yogi Tea Company had attached to the tea bag the phrase, "The purpose of life is to enjoy every moment."

United States Army General Stanley McChrystal (former commander of international forces in Afghanistan), when once asked if he could put anything on a billboard, what would it be, responded, "The purpose of life is a life of purpose."[6]

XPRIZE founder Peter Diamandis' morning meditation breathing ritual involves saying the words, "I see, hear, feel, and know that the purpose of my life is to inspire and guide the transformation of humanity on and off the earth."[7]

All three of these quotes have something in common: the speaker believes that one's purpose in life is to *do* something. One's purpose in life is to carry out some sort of action or achieve a certain result.

Yogi Tea believes people *should be* enjoying life, McChrystal believes people *should be* living life with goals, and Diamandis believes people (or at least he) *should be* inspiring and transforming people. Their analyses of the meaning of life involve imperative verbs. As opposed to describing the meaning of life with a simple *declarative* (the meaning of life is X), now we're describing the meaning of life with an *imperative* snuck in (the meaning of life is *do X*). This grammar is of unimaginable importance.

Maybe without even thinking of it, when we describe the meaning of life in these terms, we are saying that life has some type of transcendentally or objectively good purpose. That is, there's a right way and a wrong way to live. According to Yogi Tea, you are doing the *right* thing if you make the choices in life that give you the opportunity to enjoy life and you are doing the *wrong* thing if you don't make those choices. According to McChrystal, you are doing the *right* thing if you strive for goals and you are doing the *wrong* thing if you don't have any goals in life.

Sometimes we share in this thinking. I was counseling a young man named Luc who was between things. He had finished college but hadn't landed a job. He kept saying, "My life has no meaning." What he *meant* was clear: "There's something I *ought to be doing.*" Or think of a related situation. I had a father in my office seeking advice on how to counsel his son, Mark. Mark, like Luc, had finished college and didn't yet have a job. The difference, though, was that Mark wasn't looking for a job. He was content to sit at home, play video games, and watch shows. His dad kept saying, "How can Mark live such a meaningless life? We didn't teach him that way." What the father *meant* was clear: "There's something Mark *ought to be doing.*" In both cases, the language of meaning was being used to express a sort of ethical principle: The right way to live is to do something productive with your life, and the wrong way to live is to *not* be pursuing a productive life. In some sense, Mark was doing something *wrong*. Mark's dad and Luc both seemed to believe, to some degree, that the purpose of life is a life of purpose. Did you catch this subtle slide into ethical language, the language of directives and intentions? As soon as you say, "There's something I *ought to be doing*," you have stepped into the realm of ethics. Now you are asking an ethical or moral question, because if you are trying to define your purpose in life and you say there are things you *ought* to be doing, then there are things you *ought not* to be doing (just like Mark's dad thought). That's why we'll call this expressing belief in a *moral meaning* of life.

Now, all things being equal, there's nothing inherently wrong with talking like this. It's natural to begin describing meaning in life in these moral, ethical, actionable terms. What's interesting, though, is asking the questions, *Why do I need to live like that? Who says life is given to me to enjoy or create goals?* Mark could easily say to his dad, "Where did this *ethical* principle of yours come from, that I need to be doing something productive with my life?" *Who gives you the right to say that I'm not living the correct way if I don't do these things?* And so, logically, in order to talk about life having moral meaning, the universe also has to have what we call *cosmic* meaning, that is, a framework or overarching reason from which this ethic flows. And it's this final definition of meaning that we turn to last.

COSMIC MEANING *AND* METANARRATIVE

To say the world has *cosmic* meaning is to say there's an overall meaning or purpose to the universe. We aren't talking about how the universe got here but what the universe is here *for*. The former is simply describing a chain of events (a Big Bang, a six-day creation, etc.); the latter is describing the motivation or purposeful will *behind* whatever chain of events brought about this universe.

To say that the universe has cosmic meaning is to say that it has what we'll call a *metanarrative*. A metanarrative is simply an overarching or transcendent story or idea within which all other stories or ideas fit and are legitimized or explained. As many chapters make up a book, think of your life as a chapter in the book of this universe. The plot of the book is the metanarrative. An understanding of the plot of a book helps you come to grips with why what's happening to the characters in a specific chapter is significant. Analogously, understanding the metanarrative of the universe (if it, indeed, has one) helps you come to grips with why what's happening to *you* and everyone else in this universe is significant.

Of course, some people believe the universe *doesn't have* a metanarrative, that there's no "plot" to speak of that runs through this universe. Some believe the universe just *is,* and whatever happens before or after your "chapter" isn't planned, arranged, or written in any intelligent way. (Some philosophers would say the world still has a metanarrative; it's just one void of narrative!) Let's look at these differing views of the universe in detail.

GAME OF THRONES

Many works of literature presuppose a philosophy of the meaning of life and have their own understandings of the metanarrative of this universe built into them. Let's compare two bits of narrative from two very different stories and notice two very different metanarratives. Consider what these excerpts tell us about the overall world within each story, the overall principles and guiding philosophies. The first is an excerpt from George R. R. Martin's book *A Game of Thrones.*

> Frog-faced Lord Slynt sat at the end of the council table wearing a black velvet doublet and a shiny cloth-of-gold cape, nodding with approval every time the king pronounced a sentence. Sansa stared hard at his ugly face, remembering how he had thrown down her father for Ser Ilyn to behead, wishing she could hurt him, wishing that some hero would throw him down and cut off his head. But a voice inside her whispered, *There are no heroes,* and she remembered what Lord Petyr had said to her, here in this

very hall. *"Life is not a song, sweetling,"* he'd told her. *"You may learn that one day to your sorrow."* *In life, the monsters win.* (emphasis added)

Martin is famous for giving us a world in *A Game of Thrones* in which there is little hope or transcendent purpose or meaning. The sections I've italicized help shed light on this story's metanarrative: "There are no heroes" and "the monsters win," which mean the characters cannot assume they will be rescued and live happily ever after. "Life is not a song," that is, life is not beautiful or poetic but rather crass and ugly, and so we shouldn't be surprised or let down when we experience its crass nature or ugliness—as Sansa experiences in her present and future sufferings. Although the series is not complete, we experience the metanarrative for *A Game of Thrones* in what's written so far: the universe does not have any real purpose or direction, there's a good deal of evil that simply flourishes and will never be accounted for, and there's no real moral purpose to speak of other than simply trying to survive.

And Martin himself basically believes this is what the real world (outside of *A Game of Thrones*) is like. Given the amount of suffering and the lack of upbeat endings to his story arcs, Martin was asked whether his books are cynical about human nature. He responded, "I think the books are realistic."[8] Citing examples of real life "red weddings" and the like, he has given the impression often enough that he believes the world you and I live in is a world where there is no overarching *good* story on a trajectory toward a happy ending.

Now compare Martin's world with that of another popular fantasy book series:

LORD OF THE RINGS

J. R. R. Tolkien's *The Lord of the Rings* is the story of Frodo and Sam, two hobbits (little, humanlike creatures) who are on a quest to destroy a powerful evil artifact, a magical ring. Although small and rather harmless compared to the epic forces in the rest of the story, against all odds (spoiler alert!) the hobbits are successful. But there are many moments of weakness and doubting within the story, when the two friends consider whether they can make it. Here's one of these moments (captured in the film *The Two Towers*):

Frodo: I can't do this, Sam.

Sam: I know. It's all wrong. By rights we shouldn't even be here. But we are. It's like in the great stories, Mr. Frodo. The ones that really mattered. Full of darkness and danger they were, and sometimes you didn't want to know the end. Because how could the end be happy? How could the world go back to the way it was when so much bad happened? But in the end, it's only a passing thing, this shadow. Even darkness must pass. A new day will come. And when the sun shines, it will shine out the clearer. Those were the stories that stayed with you. That meant something. Even if you were too small to understand why. But I think, Mr. Frodo, I do understand. I know now. Folk in those stories had lots of chances of turning back, only they didn't. They kept going. Because they were holding on to something.

Frodo: What are we holding on to, Sam?

Sam: That there's some good in this world, Mr. Frodo. And it's worth fighting for.

First, notice the similarities between Martin's story and Tolkien's. Both involve the existence of evil and moments when evil seems to have the upper hand. Both involve comparatively weak characters (the young girl Sansa and two small hobbits) facing enormous evil and experiencing enormous suffering.

But also note the differences. In Martin's world, our hopes are dashed over and over again, and we are left more often than not with the impression that the forces of good will fail, the monsters will win, and there are no heroes that will deliver a good ending. In Tolkien's world, Sam encourages his friend, "There's some good in this world, Mr. Frodo. And it's worth fighting for." Tolkien's metanarrative is radically different from Martin's. In Tolkien's world, there is a grand war being fought between the forces of good and evil, *and good wins*. Although evil has its moments, it will be accounted for.

And the reason good ultimately wins is because the universe of *The Lord of the Rings* was created by a powerful godlike entity for a good purpose. Whereas Martin declares life is not a song, Tolkien's universe portrays literally the exact opposite. In *The Silmarillion* (Tolkien's book that gives the account of the creation of his fantastical world of Middle Earth), Illuvatar, the creator, actually declares as he makes the universe, "I will now that ye make in harmony together a Great Music." Evil, then, is compared to dissonant sounds meant to destroy the song, but the creator weaves the dissonance into the song to make minor chords and musical accents that actually make the music *more* beautiful.

Whether or not you think Tolkien's metanarrative in any way reflects the universe you live in, the point is that his world has a metanarrative involving a universe created for a good purpose to have a good ending. And the characters within his universe discover cosmic meaning in life insofar as they discover their roles in helping to bring about that good ending. Martin's world is the opposite. His universe was not created for a good purpose to have a good ending. And so the characters within the universe cannot discover cosmic meaning in life because they cannot be sure they will contribute toward any good ending. They're simply trying to survive.

NATURE AND METANARRATIVE

We have now covered enough ground that we can return to the words of the Teacher. At first blush, the Teacher seems to fall more on Martin's side than Tolkien's. (We'll have to see if that's where he stays.) After his striking opening statement that everything is utterly meaningless, the Teacher shares a poem about the ebb and flow of the natural world. He uses nature as proof that life can easily appear to be something like the world of Martin's *A Game of Thrones*. Try to pick up the emotion the Teacher wants to convey in these opening lines of his treatise:

> "Meaningless! Meaningless!"
>   says the Teacher.
>
> "Utterly meaningless!
>   Everything is meaningless."
>
> What do people gain from all their labors
>   at which they toil under the sun?
>
> Generations come and generations go,
>   but the earth remains forever.
>
> The sun rises and the sun sets,
>   and hurries back to where it rises.
>
> The wind blows to the south
>   and turns to the north;
>
> round and round it goes,
>   ever returning on its course.
>
> All streams flow into the sea,
>   yet the sea is never full.
>
> To the place the streams come from,
>   there they return again.
>
> All things are wearisome,
>   more than one can say.
>
> The eye never has enough of seeing,
>   nor the ear its fill of hearing.

What has been will be again,
  what has been done will be done again;
  there is nothing new under the sun.

Is there anything of which one can say,
  "Look! This is something new"?

It was here already, long ago;
  it was here before our time.[9]

How is the Teacher describing nature? Is this poetry meant to praise nature's beauty, complexity, and awe-inspiring qualities? Actually, quite the opposite seems to be happening. Nature is described in terms of an eternal weariness and monotony, void of any real progress or goal or end. Rivers eternally empty into the sea, and yet the sea never fills up. The wind blows on and on and never seems to end. Our senses go on seeing and hearing and smelling and never stop. And so the Teacher complains, "All things are wearisome, more than one can say."

Maybe you've experienced the weary monotony of the forces of life, maybe not. But I think you will one day. You will wake up in the morning just as you always have, and the daily grind will begin. And even if you decide to take the day off, the world will continue to grind on without you, never stopping, your inbox continually filling whether or not you empty it. You will end one day finishing one to-do list, just to wake up the next morning with a new to-do list, and the next day a new one, and the next day a new one.

Do you feel it? Life can seem a weary, pointless place, with the monotony of the entire planet seeming to write large that the metanarrative of our lives is something like that of Martin's world—a universe with little direction or purpose. Things just go on, keep happening, with no real goal, no end in sight. Our world doesn't *look* like a story with an ending, with a final chapter, with the good conclusion it's striving for.

The Teacher deepens this idea with an observation he will make several more times in his book: "No one remembers the former generations, and even those yet to come will not be remembered by those who follow them."[10] Because of the weary march of time toward nothing in particular, what we do as humans in this weary world lacks any real meaning or long-term value. Recall our discussions on short-term value. A time will come, the Teacher is saying, when whatever it is you do today will be forgotten. It doesn't matter how big or important it seems, the march of time will inevitably leave you and your accomplishments behind forever, never to be considered again.

In short, the Teacher asks us to imagine a world in which a purposeful, overarching metanarrative does not exist. What's that world like? There is no cosmic meaning, and so there is no moral meaning: There is no way one *should* live life, because nothing we do really matters if it will all be forgotten. Nothing really matters if the world goes on regardless of what I do or say today. Nothing really matters if "generations come and generations go, but the earth remains forever." And so the Teacher declares it all *meaningless*. The old Hebrew word we translate here as *meaningless* in other contexts is translated *breath* or *vapor*. Just as an exhaled breath is fleeting, intangible, quickly forgotten, so are the days of our lives "under the sun."

And we don't want to hear this, obviously. But we need to.

And if we don't hear it from the Teacher, we'll hear it from songs like "Broken Chair." Or Peggy Lee asking, "Is That All There Is?" (a song President Donald Trump once mentioned was his favorite). Or Queen's "Bohemian Rhapsody" crooning, "Nothing really matters." Or Smashing Pumpkins' "Bullet With Butterfly Wings" declaring, "The world is a vampire, sent to drain." Or Foo Fighters' "Saint Cecilia" chiming in, "I know no matter what I say days will come and go." So don't be surprised if you catch yourself humming a rather catchy nihilistic tune, because our art is on to it.

Even more explicitly, we can hear the Teacher's message from some of the more notable thinkers of our modern age. And to the most infamous of these thinkers we turn next.

NIETZSCHE AND THE MADMAN

Near the end of the 19th century, as the Statue of Liberty was being built, as pogroms began to sweep through Russia, and as Mark Twain and Oscar Wilde were penning their works, a German philosopher, Friedrich Nietzsche, infamously wrote the phrase *"God is dead."* But what he meant by that is often deeply misunderstood. Nietzsche was an atheist, but he was not an atheist evangelist. When he wrote, "God is dead," he wasn't trying to convince anyone that they should stop believing in God. (He did that in other writings, just not the one in which this phrase first occurred.) It was his dramatic way of saying that life had no meaning, no metanarrative, now that the usefulness of God as a concept was past. The *idea* of God among intellectuals was dead. Academia had left God behind. And Nietzsche was terrified at the implications of this.

How had God been left behind by academia?

During this time period, Darwinist evolution was becoming all the rage as it attempted to explain the origin of human life *apart* from the need of a Creator-God. In philosophy, thinkers like Immanuel Kant had declared that ethics could be given a foundation *apart* from God. In art, English and German romantic poets and musicians and visual artists had largely left religious concerns behind and now created art *apart* from the context of the Christian God. In a nutshell, there was really no need for God in academic life anymore.

But was this okay?

Nietzsche didn't think so. He believed we had no clue what implications leaving God behind would have. And so, to try to impress on our minds how we ought to prepare ourselves for the fallout of a now-godless world, he wrote a famous parable:

> Have you not heard of that madman who lit a lantern in the bright morning hours, ran to the market place, and cried incessantly: "I seek God! I seek God!"—As many of those who did not believe in God were standing around just then, he provoked much laughter. . . .
>
> The madman jumped into their midst and pierced them with his eyes. "Whither is God?" he cried; "I will tell you. We have killed him—you and I. All of us are his murderers. But how did we do this? How could we drink up the sea? Who gave us the sponge to wipe away the entire horizon? What were we doing when we unchained this earth from its sun? Whither is it moving now? Whither are we moving? Away from all suns? Are we not plunging continually? Backward, sideward, forward, in all directions? Is there still any up or down? Are we not straying, as through an infinite nothing? Do we not feel the breath of empty space? Has it not become colder? Is not night continually closing in on us? Do we not need to light lanterns in the morning? . . . There has never been a greater deed; and whoever is born after us—for the sake of this deed he will belong to a higher history than all history hitherto."
>
> Here the madman fell silent and looked again at his listeners; and they, too, were silent and stared at him in astonishment. At last he threw his lantern on the ground, and it broke into pieces and went out. "I have come too early," he said then; "my time is not yet. This tremendous event is still on its way, still wandering; it has not yet reached the ears of men. Lightning and thunder require time."[11]

Notice a few things: First, as mentioned, Nietzsche is not trying here to convince anyone that God is dead. The madman in the parable has burst into a scene where everyone *already* does not believe in God. Nietzsche's parable shocks, not with the revelation that God is dead but rather the revelation that *only one person, a madman,* thinks it's important! Everyone else believes that life without God is fine. But the madman doesn't think so. By thinking we can get on without God, he tells us, we have somehow wiped away the horizon and unchained the earth from its sun. In other words, we have lost a frame of reference: We can no longer tell if we're moving in any direction; we can no longer tell up from down.

Nietzsche is speaking metaphorically, of course. What he means (using some of the language we've established earlier) is that without God to provide a *metanarrative,* we now find ourselves in a world with no *cosmic* meaning and no *moral* meaning. We are adrift in the universe. If God did not create us (if we are only the products of genetic mutations and natural selection), we were not created for a reason; we are just here. If God did not create us to live a certain way, no one can talk about what you should or should not do with your life. If something has come about by mindless processes, it cannot by definition have any purpose. Purpose arises only from a *mind,* like the mind of God. If there is no God, literally, "Meaningless! Meaningless! . . . Everything is meaningless."

Again, this parable was meant to be a commentary on the *implications* of the death of God. Philosophers and theologians in the 1800s believed that life could continue along pretty much as it always had in the wake of the disposal of God, but Nietzsche was arguing that the implications would be enormous and would require drastic changes to the way we live. Nietzsche's world had not felt the shock waves of God's death yet. But when they finally would feel them, Nietzsche wrote elsewhere that night would then close in and "an age of barbarism begins" and "there will be wars such as have never happened on earth."

If it sounds like Nietzsche was predicting the world wars of the 20th century, you could very well be right. In this sense, Nietzsche strove to be a prophet, predicting a world unable to cope with the loss of our foundation for cosmic meaning, purpose, and ethics. Life without a *metanarrative,* life considered apart from a

Creator-God, is like "straying, as through an infinite nothing," a darkness void of anything transcendent to give lasting meaning and purpose to our lives.

Nietzsche's madman declares, "I have come too early." Today, though, we are in a perfect position to experience and discuss the repercussions (as my students constantly demonstrate).

INCREDULITY TOWARD A METANARRATIVE

Today we feel the breath of empty space. Today many have embraced Nietzsche's (and so also the Teacher's) view of the world becoming philosophically and morally colder.

Stephen Sondheim brilliantly captured this in his musical *Into the Woods*. In fact, this musical eerily seems to follow our discussions too closely. The musical is separated into two acts.

The first tells the story of several familiar fairy-tale characters, like Jack and his beanstalk, princes saving princesses, and Little Red Riding Hood. There is a narrator who tells how each one sets out on his or her own quest—these individual quests all weaving into one overarching story. Near the end of the act, the narrator describes how everything has more or less come to a good ending.

But then, during the second act, something incredible happens: The narrator is sacrificed to a giant. Now there is no more narrator's voice, and things end very differently in the second act. The princes turn out to be misogynistic, womanizing jerks. Characters, like a witch, who had been clearly bad in the first act now become more morally ambiguous. And people die. Lots of people. All in the silence of an un-narrated story. At one point, a character breaks out into song:

> **Mother cannot guide you.**
> **Now you're on your own,**
> **Only me beside you.**
> **Still, you're not alone. . . .**

> Everybody makes
> One another's terrible mistakes.
> Witches can be right.
> Giants can be good.
> You decide what's right.
> You decide what's good.

The message ought to be clear to us. In a world with no "narrator," no metanarrative accessible to us, no godlike omniscient perspective that gives perspective to everything else, we find ourselves alone, suffering, and directionless. There is no discoverable right or wrong; you just have to decide it for yourself. There's no good or bad; we're all just grey. We can't look to the wisdom of the past or to others (like our parents) to ultimately help us; we're all just as lost. This musical ends rather darkly, with no one really knowing quite how to go on and everyone finding themselves in, as Nietzsche describes, a cold and continual night devoid of direction and purpose. The Disney adaptation tried to wrap things up on a positive note with a beautiful major key song underlying the final moments, but the sweet music was jarringly juxtaposed with the camera panning out on a widowed baker holding a child with no mother surrounded by what only could be described as a war-torn battlefield.

I often use *Into the Woods* as my students' introduction to 20th-century continental (European) philosophy. As the angst of the musical begins to sink in, my students begin asking questions like, "If you're on your own, how do you know if you're going the right way?"

"If two people disagree on what's good, which one is right?"

"How can I tell whether what the witch is saying is wrong or right?"

And then I know we're exactly where we need to be. Because the truth is that the main themes of Sondheim's play are the main themes with which many contemporary thinkers have been wrestling.

Step into any philosophy classroom to discuss what happened in 20th-century continental (European) philosophy and you will find a world of thinkers surrounded by a vacuum, an emptiness of values and objectivity. Philosophers will carefully label many continental movements and schools of thought (maybe you've heard of atheistic existentialism, ethical relativism, structuralism, deconstruction-ism, or other related movements), but we can understand most of them as variations of the same tune we'll call postmodernism. And Jean-Francois Lyotard, one of the key figures in French postmodern thought, labels postmodernism best for our purposes with the famous (at least to philosophers) phrase, "I define postmodern as incredulity toward metanarratives."[12] Postmodernism is, in effect, the belief that there is no overarching story that applies to all people in all places.[13] The idea of interpreting the whole world through, for example, a religious framework of a God or gods creating the world is to be rejected completely. If there is no God, there is no overarching story of which we're all a part. There are only our individual stories and perspectives and opinions or, at best, the stories, perspectives, and opinions of communities.

The implication, then, is that there is no overarching ethic to guide all humans. A whole generation of philosophers has thus embraced Nietzsche's claim that there is no metanarrative and that we need to learn how to get on without it. Yet, this death of God produces tremendous difficulties for knowing morally in which direction we're moving. As Sondheim sings "You decide," without a metanarrative, our traditional guides are gone, our traditional understanding of good and evil needs to be rethought, and, whatever conclusions we come to, it's hard to see how they are anything more than our own opinions. The philosopher Alasdair MacIntyre puts his finger on the issue this way:

> I can only answer the question "What am I to do?" if I can answer the prior question "Of what story or stories do I find myself a part?"[14]

It could be argued that Sondheim's musical is meant to be liberating, to show us what life is really like, and to inspire us to dive bravely into the ambiguity and grey spectrum of morality and meaning. But that's not how I feel every time I watch the musical. And that's not how my students generally feel after they slow down to think through what's happening. We feel sad, knowing that so many are drifting through life feeling just as lost as these characters—lost in the postmodern woods of this world. Sondheim describes life "under the sun," as the Teacher calls it, apart from a purpose-driven metanarrative, and it can be a cold and lonely life to live. All I want to do is stand up and call out to my fellow theatergoers, "We are in a *good* story! There *is* direction and purpose and meaning to it all. And I know this because I have heard the voice of the Narrator. He's not dead. You're just not listening."

OVER THE SUN?

Now I have shown my hand, so to speak. I personally believe God is not dead. The Narrator is not dead. His name is Jesus. He is very much a part of my life right now. He loves me. And I love him.

And yet I still agree with the Teacher, one hundred percent.

Although the Teacher's message of meaninglessness sounds so much like Nietzsche's, Martin's, and Sondheim's, what sets the Teacher apart from them is that somehow he got his book included in the Bible. His masterpiece Ecclesiastes (from a Greek word for *Teacher*, or *Qohelet* in the Hebrew) is included as one of the holiest writings of the Jewish and Christian traditions. It was most certainly in the Bible that Jesus read.

But not everyone has wanted it in the Bible. For example, the *Pesikta de-Rav Kahana*, a collection of Jewish *midrash,* or homilies, originating in early medieval times, famously says, "The sages sought to store away the Book of Ecclesiastes, because they found words in it which tended to heresy."[15] On the Christian side, we might consider the words of the prominent 19th-century Hebraist Dr. Franz Delitzsch, who wrote concerning Ecclesiastes that a Christian "would not be able to write such a book." He went so far as to call it "the darkness of earth" written down amid "heaps of ruins."[16]

While many Christians read the book "with the distinct feeling that [it] does not belong in the Bible,"[17] atheists have welcomed its presence in the biblical canon. In a 2016 post entitled "A Book of the Bible Even an Atheist Can Love," Jeffrey Tayler writes for the blog of the *Los Angeles Review of Books* that Ecclesiastes is

> a book of the Old Testament that I, an atheist with an ardent distaste for religion, find consoling, calming, and wise. As the years pass and cares mount, as pleasures fade with repetition, and as the senescence and deaths of family members bear down relentlessly, I find myself turning to Ecclesiastes for comfort, inspiration, and, despite its melancholy tidings, cheer. . . . Luckily, *Ecclesiastes* barely mentions God. When it does, the words seem almost pro forma, as though the author had suddenly thought, "Hey, I better at least nod to the Lord or they won't put my book in the Bible!"[18]

I think Tayler rightly praises Ecclesiastes. I'm happy it's in the Bible too, and I also find it encouraging. And for ten years, many of the students I've worked with as a philosophy professor and Christian pastor have also found the book encouraging. But I also think, far from *pro forma,* it fits perfectly in the biblical canon, and I think the Teacher and Jesus would have gotten along brilliantly.

Let me share with you the main insight that has most helped my students and me to see where the Teacher very intentionally left a place for hope in a writing that could easily be mistaken as skeptical and nihilistic. Up to this point, we have been entertaining what life is like "under the sun," because this is where the Teacher wants us to begin. He wants us to struggle with what life looks like if we have no larger-than-life metanarrative. He wants the first words ringing in our ears to be that life is meaningless "under the sun." And as we will see, his masterpiece Ecclesiastes is a study of this truth from most every angle possible. The Teacher (with help from Nietzsche) has so far laid out for us the general truth that without God *every-thing* loses its cosmic meaning. Through the following chapters of Ecclesiastes (and so in the following chapters of this book), we'll look more closely at specific things that lose their cosmic meaning: the accumulation of knowledge, the pursuit of a pleasurable life, work and labor, and, ultimately, the value of human life itself.

The Teacher uses the phrase "under the sun" 27 times in his rela-tively brief work. He means to constantly draw our gaze downward to the world around us, the world as it appears, as we experience it empirically. But I am convinced that he doesn't mean to keep us looking down here. He dins that refrain "under the sun" into our ears so that we might ask, "What if there's a place *over the sun,* beyond this world's light?" The Teacher draws our gaze downward because he eventually wants to draw our gaze upward to compare what life is like *with* and *without* the overarching story of which he believes we're a part.

And within what metanarrative *does* the Teacher want us to pic-ture our world? What grand story can renew our hope? The Teacher believed it was the grand Story of the rest of the Bible, the Story that the Teacher learned as a toddler on his mother's knee. The most precious characteristic of the Teacher's book, I would say, is the way that he looks all the world's bleakness square in the face and yet still holds on to that Story. And that Story might go something like this:

This world was created for a good purpose, by a good God. He *is* goodness and love. He created humankind so that he could spend all the eons to come loving them. And he cre-ated a perfect world designed just for them: a world perfect for scientists, artists, explorers; a world perfect for socializing communities and more personal meditation and reflection.

But all too soon, forces of evil arose. A great enemy arose, a liar and murderer. Out of hatred for God and God's love, he convinced humankind it was better to play God than be loved by God. This rebellion against their Creator brought into the world strife, ruin, depravity, and estrangement from God.

The great Story of our universe, then, is the unfolding of God's plan to both defeat the enemy and his forces of evil *and* rescue as many as possible. God promised humankind since the beginning that he would rescue them (promises that the Teacher would have been raised on). The climax of this Story is God's rescue, his entering his own creation, entering our history, in the person of Jesus. Jesus broke the enemy's power over humanity's estrangement from God. Through this great act of love, God made loving him possible again.

This infuses life with epic meaning, as God lets us share in his work of undoing the world's strife, ruin, and depravity. He calls those who have found freedom in this rescue to love those around them as he has loved them.

Set aside for a moment any philosophical questions of working out how all of this Story can make sense (questions like, "If God created a perfect world, where did evil come from?" or "How can God both be merciful toward those rebelling against him *and* vanquish evil?" or "The Bible has too many contradictions to say it's one big Story, doesn't it?"). Working out the logic or coherence of God's plan of salvation is important, but it is a different task entirely.

What we're interested in is how this metanarrative shapes who you are and what you do daily, and how its cosmic meaning and purpose infuses what you are doing right now with meaning and purpose. Compare how radically different the implications are compared with Nietzsche's madman's world. When you consider your life not "under the sun" but rather *over the sun* or *in light of God's transcendent plan,* you will discover that you were created by a loving God who wants you to be in communion with him. And so your life has eternal value because an eternal God values you, despite how anyone else might treat you. Despite how dim things might seem at times (like in Frodo and Sam's story), you know that there is a God in control of all things, working out the hardships in your life for a grand, good ending. Despite how mundane life may seem at times, you can remind yourself you are *really* part of something far more grand, a Story involving colossal forces of good and evil. See how this metanarrative, this overarching Story, changes everything? If you're not convinced yet, I think in the following chapters the Teacher will help me convince you how valuable this Story is.

Under the sun, apart from God in a cosmic sense, life is most certainly meaningless. Without him, this world is a jumbled collection of words gathered together into random heaps of meaningless pages and chapters.

But this focus on life "under the sun" is really an invitation to view the world from God's side of it, from over and beyond the sun. You will find an epic Story of love, warfare, salvation, and heroism; you will find a beginning, a tragic fall, a climax, and a good ending waiting for us; and you will find your own name on those pages, playing out your part.

———————•———————

two

WISDOM IS
MEANINGLESS

———•———

"I believe we *can* construct meaning. Suppose science *does* tell us there's no mind behind the big bang. We just need to deal with it. And I think we can." My friend works for the Canadian federal government as a scientist. He's brilliant. There's no denying it. He's also a committed atheist. I asked him how it might be possible to construct meaning, and he answered with one word: "Science." As he began to explain his answer, he sounded an awful lot like another scientist, one I do not know on a first-name basis.

Neil deGrasse Tyson—the scientist, public speaker, and promoter of science and astronomy—once spoke to a group of parents and children in a question-and-answer session. At one point, a six-year-old asked Tyson what is the meaning of life. He responded:

> I think people ask that question on the assumption that meaning is something you can look for and then, "Oh I found it. . . ." And it doesn't consider the possibility that maybe meaning in life is something that you create. . . . And so when I think of meaning in life, I ask, "Am I learning something today that I didn't know yesterday?" bringing me a little closer to knowing

all that can be known in the universe. . . . If I live a day and I don't know a little more that day than the day before, I think I wasted that day. . . . Your meaning in life will be enhanced if you are given as much freedom as you can to explore the world. Then, when you get older, you will become so close to how the world works, that when a problem arises that needs a solution, you will say, "I know how to solve that; I've been thinking about that before. . . . " You owe it to yourself and everyone else to continue to stay curious, and by doing so you will have created meaning in life that others think is waiting under a rock for them one day, and you would have made it happen all on your own.[19]

Let's call to mind some of our ways of talking about meaning as sketched out in our previous chapter and note the way Tyson is talking about the meaning of life. First, he believes, like my friend, that meaning in life is something that can be *created*. So he is clearly talking about *short-term* meaning, not cosmic meaning. Remember, short-term meaning is meaning that arises from temporal individuals like ourselves simply giving value to certain things or people or activities, but once all the persons giving value to these things are gone, the value disappears with them.

This certainly applies to science. Imagine some long-lost civilization; we'll call it Atlantis. In Atlantis there is a scientist that makes a tremendous discovery: how to turn lead into gold. He values this discovery, this accumulation of knowledge, and so does his civilization around him. But then Atlantis sinks into the sea, along with the scientist and his textbooks and his diagrams and all the people that knew about this discovery, never to be seen again. What else dies with this city? Any value or meaning that flowed from this discovery. If the universe is billions of years old, as many scientists believe, the existence of this discovery and the people it affected is a blink of an eye in the universe's history. Things go on after this discovery pretty much as they had before. The meaning derived from scientific discovery is *short-term:* It has value for those it affects (either directly or indirectly), maybe even *tremendous* value (such as a cure for a disease you personally have), but it is still contingent on people to value it and therefore has a lifespan. This doesn't mean science isn't a meaningful vocation. We can certainly use the words *meaning* and *knowledge* in the same sentence. Let's just note that science can't somehow create *cosmic* meaning—something fixed and permanent and applicable to the entire universe, something that answers the question, "Why are we here?"

However, this doesn't stop Tyson from seeing a *purpose* in human existence. That purpose is clearly to do science: to accumulate empirical knowledge ("Am I learning something today that I didn't know yesterday?") and to apply that knowledge practically ("When a problem arises that needs a solution, you will say, 'I know how to solve that'"). This means Tyson clearly believes there's a *moral* meaning to life, an imperative, something people ought to *do*, and if they're not doing it, they're in a sense being immoral or, in his own words, *wasting* life. This is a common enough way of thinking of the meaning of life in our own time (especially given the prevalence of subtle *scientism*, the view that the only thing that counts as true knowledge is scientific knowledge).

But if Tyson tells you that this is how you *should* live your life, how might you respond? "Why?" "Who are *you* to tell me how I ought to live?" "How do you know this is the purpose of human existence?" Moral meaning is always contingent on cosmic meaning—an overarching metanarrative from which purpose in life flows. I would love to ask Tyson if he thinks this universe has any cosmic meaning. If he thinks not, where does his moral imperative to do science come from?

The accumulation of knowledge, honing its applications as ends in themselves, considering advancement in understanding to be the meaning of life—none of this is anything particularly new. In fact, the first topic the Teacher in Ecclesiastes fixates on (after declaring that life in general "under the sun" has no cosmic meaning) is this very thing. Can you sense the common bond the author once had with Tyson in his pursuit for wisdom?

> I, the Teacher, was king over Israel in Jerusalem. I applied my mind to study and to explore by wisdom all that is done under the heavens. What a heavy burden God has laid on mankind! I have seen all the things that are done under the sun; all of them are meaningless, a chasing after the wind.
>
>> What is crooked cannot be straightened;
>> what is lacking cannot be counted.
>
> I said to myself, "Look, I have increased in wisdom more than anyone who has ruled over Jerusalem before me; I have experienced much of wisdom and knowledge." Then I applied myself to the understanding of wisdom, and also of madness and folly, but I learned that this, too, is a chasing after the wind.
>
>> For with much wisdom comes much sorrow;
>> the more knowledge, the more grief.[20]

Even after describing a life lived in pursuit of wisdom, the Teacher declares that *everything* done under the sun is meaningless. And he's in an interesting position to comment on what the accumulation of knowledge amounts to. Now might be a good time to consider in detail just who this author is claiming to be.

SOLOMON, THE PHILOSOPHER KING

I don't know what you think about taking the Bible as a historically reliable collection of very real events or whether you think it fits into real ancient history, but right now the important thing is that the author of Ecclesiastes wants us to at least *imagine* that he is King Solomon. All right, so let's imagine.

Perhaps you've heard of David and Goliath. That is a story from the Bible from the early life of King David, who was (again, according to the historical accounts in the Bible) the second king of the ancient nation of Israel. David lived approximately 1010 to 970 B.C. After many great military conquests, David passed on his throne to his son Solomon. Solomon is said to have ruled over Israel at the peak of its prosperity and power, from roughly 970 to 930 B.C. The most memorable event in the Bible's biographies of Solomon's life is most certainly the following account recorded in 1 Kings 3:

> At Gibeon the LORD appeared to Solomon during the night in a dream, and God said, "Ask for whatever you want me to give you."
>
> Solomon answered, "You have shown great kindness to your servant, my father David, because he was faithful to you and righteous and upright in heart. You have continued this great kindness to him and have given him a son to sit on his throne this very day.
>
> "Now, LORD my God, you have made your servant king in place of my father David. But I am only a little child and do not know how to carry out my duties. Your servant is here among the people you have chosen, a great people, too numerous to count or number. So give your servant a discerning heart to govern your people and to distinguish between right and wrong. For who is able to govern this great people of yours?"
>
> The Lord was pleased that Solomon had asked for this. So God said to him, "Since you have asked for this and not for long life or wealth for yourself, nor have asked for the death of your enemies but for discernment in administoring jus- tice, I will do what you have asked. I will give you a wise and discerning heart, so that there will never have been anyone like you, nor will there ever be. Moreover, I will give you what you have not asked for—both wealth and honor—so that in your lifetime you will have no equal among kings. And if you walk in obedience to me and keep my decrees and com- mands as David your father did, I will give you a long life." (1 Kings 3:5-14)

This is the story into which the Teacher puts himself. This is the corner of Israel's imagination he wants to enter.

Of all things, Solomon asks for wisdom, and God grants him this to the point of saying, "There will never have been anyone like you, nor will there ever be." In other words, God is making Solomon the wisest person to ever live. And the rest of the Bible treats him as such. Three books in the Bible are attributed to him: Proverbs, a book of wisdom on how to live (Solomon didn't write the whole book but most of it); Song of Songs (sometimes called Song of Solomon), a romantic book on the beauty of erotic love within a biblical context; and Ecclesiastes, which we're studying now, a book on where cosmic meaning in life can be found. And so, the Bible's three most practical books (treatises on living, romance, and finding meaning in daily life) are said to have been penned by Solomon, whom Bible believers call the wisest man who ever lived.

Besides being a wise writer, his Bible biographies say that Solomon was known as an amazing judge (read 1 Kings 3:16-28 for the most famous example of his courtroom wisdom) and scientist. Consider the following description 1 Kings gives us:

> God gave Solomon wisdom and very great insight, and a breadth of understanding as measureless as the sand on the seashore. Solomon's wisdom was greater than the wisdom of all the people of the East, and greater than all the wisdom of Egypt. He was wiser than anyone else, including Ethan the Ezrahite—wiser than Heman, Kalcol and Darda, the sons of Mahol. And his fame spread to all the surrounding nations. He spoke three thousand proverbs and his songs numbered a thousand and five. He spoke about plant life, from the cedar of Lebanon to the hyssop that grows out of walls. He also spoke about animals and birds, reptiles and fish. From all nations people came to listen to Solomon's wisdom, sent by all the kings of the world, who had heard of his wisdom. (1 Kings 4:29-34)

And yet what did Solomon's wisdom amount to?

Despite writing *the* handbook for how to live a just and good life, Solomon often enough couldn't follow his own advice. Within the first verses of Proverbs he writes, "The fear of the LORD is the beginning of knowledge" (1:7). (The biblical concept of fear of God is this mingling of awe, love, trust, and healthy fearful recognition for God's might and strength—how a small child might feel for a good father.) Yet the Bible says he not only followed and sacrificed to other gods—including religions that demanded child sacrifice—but also built state-sponsored houses of worship for them.

In Song of Songs he weaves together beautiful language about the monogamy and exclusivity that give lifelong committed relationships the foundation upon which romance can truly flourish. "My beloved is mine and I am his" (2:16). "You are a garden locked up, my sister, my bride; you are a spring enclosed, a sealed fountain" (4:12). "I am my beloved's and my beloved is mine" (6:3). "Daughters of Jerusalem, I charge you: Do not arouse or awaken love until it so desires" (8:4). And yet Solomon has gone down in history for his hundreds of wives and concubines and for the troubles that followed him because of his clearly ungodly lifestyle.

And finally we turn to Ecclesiastes. Tradition has it that Solomon wrote this book at the end of his life, looking back at all he had accomplished, all the wealth he had gathered, all the knowledge he had learned, and all the wisdom he had taught. The emotions of an older man, now jaded from the pursuit of these things and the false belief that they would deliver something transcendentally meaningful, can be felt in every sentence. The Teacher, writing as Solomon (the most extreme example of a wise man that his culture could provide), says he learned the hard way that learning does not equal mastery. Learning *how to be good* doesn't necessarily lead to *being good*. As he says, "What is crooked cannot be straightened." And a life full of knowledge and wisdom—what Tyson might suggest is the aim of the good life—isn't necessarily a good life, whether for the wise man or those close to him. As Solomon/the Teacher says, "Then I applied myself to the understanding of wisdom, and also of madness and folly, but I learned that this, too, is a chasing after the wind."

A NOTE ON THE AUTHOR OF ECCLESIASTES

The author of Ecclesiastes identifies himself as "the son of David" and "the King in Jerusalem." Although in Hebrew, as in English, the word "son" is somewhat flexible, David only had one son who was recognized as the legitimate king in Jerusalem: Solomon. And the descriptions of the wealth, lifestyle, and education that the author gives match perfectly the unique character of King Solomon. That Solomon is the author has been the general consensus of both Jewish and Christian traditions throughout time. And so, for the remainder of this book, we'll be referring to Solomon as the author.

Yet, within this past century you'll find plenty of Hebrew scholars doubting whether there even *was* a Solomon, let alone a Solomon whom God gifted with wisdom or who wrote as the author of Ecclesiastes. For this reason, most modern scholars today will refer to the author simply as "Qohelet," the Hebrew word for "Teacher," a name which the author gives himself. It's outside of the aim of this book to address contending theories of authorship, but let's say this much: What we're going to get out of Ecclesiastes in no way rests on Solomon as the author. We'll look at Solomon's life first to see the value of Ecclesiastes, but the text itself, when treated as a single work, stands on its own merits as one of the greatest pieces of literature in history. Thomas Wolfe, the brilliant and influential American novelist who impacted the writings of Faulkner, Kerouac, Bradbury, and many others, wrote of Ecclesiastes:

> Of all I have ever seen or learned, this book seems to me the noblest, the wisest, and the most powerful expression of man's life upon this earth—and also the highest flower of poetry, eloquence, and truth. . . . Ecclesiastes is the greatest

single piece of writing I have ever known, and the wisdom expressed in it the most lasting and profound.

Wolfe's appreciation for Ecclesiastes certainly resonates with me, and I hope that by the end of this book, it will resonate with you as well. Whoever the author might be, he certainly is wise. But let's not forget what he's telling us: this great wisdom of his is "meaningless, a chasing after the wind."

DECLARATIVES CAN'T LEAD TO IMPERATIVES

The first reason "under the sun" wisdom (the knowledge gathered from scientific and philosophical inquiry) can't lead to a life of cosmic or moral meaning (that is, can't lead to knowing what one ought to do with one's life) is because of a very commonsense, yet often forgotten, truth: any observation about what the world *is* cannot logically lead to what the world *should be*. We mentioned this very briefly in our first chapter, but here we need to sketch out very precisely *why* observations can't lead to ethics. As the famous atheist philosopher David Hume would put it, an *is* cannot lead to an *ought*: what the world *is* cannot lead to how one *ought* to live. Hume put it this way:

> In every system of morality, which I have hitherto met with, I have always remark'd, that the author proceeds for some time in the ordinary way of reasoning, and establishes the being of a God, or makes observations concerning human affairs; when of a sudden I am surpriz'd to find, that instead of the usual copulations of propositions, *is*, and *is not*, I meet with no proposition that is not connected with an *ought*, or an *ought not*. This change is imperceptible; but is, however, of the last consequence. For as this *ought*, or *ought not*, expresses some new relation or affirmation, 'tis necessary that it should be observ'd and explain'd; and at the same time that a reason should be given, for what seems alto-

gether inconceivable, how this new relation can be a deduction from others, which are entirely different from it.[21]

Philosophers have famously called this *Hume's guillotine*, because he clearly severs empirical (or what we might call scientific) observations from being able to determine ethical behavior. Let's take a close look at what he writes: A thinker will begin a line of reasoning with observations, with "is" sentences. For example,

A thrush *is* a creature with feathers.
All creatures alive today with feathers *are* birds.

If both of these statements are correct, we can follow the line of reasoning from these two "is" statements (the second uses "are," the plural form of "is") to other "is" statements, such as:

A thrush *is* a bird.

Logically, "is" statements can lead to other "is" statements. That's ultimately deductive and inductive logic. But, Hume says, what we *cannot* do is move from an "is" statement to an "ought" statement ("ought" as in the sense of moral obligation). That makes no sense. Consider:

A thrush *is* a creature with feathers.
All creatures alive today with feathers *are* birds.
Therefore, a thrush *ought* to (has an obligation to) act like a bird.

Do you notice how out of place that "ought" is? No matter what we say about thrushes, we cannot get to the point where we tell the thrush what it *ought* to do (just based on observations). The thrush simply *is* or *is not* things, as far as observations and inferences on those observations go. (Note this is not an anticipatory "ought"— what we're expecting to see. This is a moral command, like telling a thrush, "This is how you *ought* to behave.") "Is" statements (that is, observations made regarding this world we live in) can't possibly lead to ethics, to knowing what a person (or animal, for that matter) *ought* to do. If you see how this clearly follows in regards to thrushes, let's see how this follows in regards to theft.

Sometimes people are not punished for stealing.
But sometimes people are punished for stealing.
Therefore, people ought not steal.

Any observations one makes about human behavior, such as stealing in this example, cannot lead to imperative propositions on how one ought to act. Just because we can observe whether or not people steal, this doesn't mean we can observe whether or not they *should* steal. Whether or not they get caught doesn't help either. In fact, plenty of people get punished for doing what we know is the right thing. (The Bible has a whole account dedicated to this: Acts 5:17-42.) We could create "ought" statements about how to bring about certain states of affairs (such as, "If one doesn't want to ever be punished for stealing, then one ought not steal"), but this is a far cry from a binding statement of ethics. It tells us nothing about whether or not stealing is wrong and thus whether one *in principle* ought to or ought not to steal. In order to answer the question, "Ought people steal?" we need to look beyond wisdom "under the sun," beyond simple statements of fact about the observable world around us. We need something that puts us in touch with the overarching metanarrative *beyond the sun.*

I personally would say that the human conscience can do this, because the conscience puts us in contact with something beyond the mere appearances of this world. In a person's conscience, God has inscribed information not found anywhere else in this world, namely, God's desire for specific human behaviors and our inability to carry out these behaviors. Besides being aware of these things from conscience, Christians believe that we can learn these things even more directly from God's own words (that is, the Bible). Apart from transcendent sources like these (conscience and the Bible), simple empirical, scientific observations about the observable world we live in could never lead to reliable knowledge about what we *ought* to do.

This is well-recognized by many nonreligious thinkers. Thomas Nagel, one of the more famous atheists at the turn of the 21st century, wrote a book titled *Mind and Cosmos*. In it he argued that scientific naturalism (the belief that this world was created by an uncaused big bang and has since developed to the point it's at today through the forces of physics and Darwinian evolution alone, nothing else) cannot account for certain features we know simply exist. Note what these features are:

> The conflict between scientific naturalism and various forms of antireductionism is a staple of recent philosophy. On one side there is the hope that everything can be accounted for at the most basic level by the physical sciences, extended to include biology. On the other side are doubts about whether the reality of such features of our world as consciousness, intentionality, meaning, purpose, thought, and value can be accommodated in a universe consisting at the most basic level of physical facts—facts, however sophisticated, of the kind revealed by the physical sciences.[22]

To summarize Nagel, physical facts (empirically observed statements of "is," we might say) cannot account for certain features of this world. In his list, he includes meaning, purpose, and value. In other words, science cannot lead to "ought" statements: You *ought* to treat human life with dignity because human life has value; you *ought* to love others or strive for a meaningful life because life has some sort of *purpose*; etc. Nagel might very well reply to Tyson, "If you want to talk about life having any transcendent, bigger-than-ourselves, morally imperative meaning, you *have* to look outside of science."

But then where do we look? Nagel, as an atheist, did not have an answer to this question. He simply stated that scientific naturalist explanations (that is, the scientific explanations many atheists would give for why the universe exists) can't do it. Science can only tell us what we, in fact, do; it can never tell us what we *ought* to do. This is the first reason "under the sun" wisdom cannot lead to moral meaning.

And so, after the Teacher writes about his increasing in wisdom and learning, he says, "I have seen all the things that are done under the sun; all of them are meaningless" (Ecclesiastes 1:14). In what sense are they meaningless? In part because simply growing in empirical knowledge about this world can't lead to discovering moral values, purpose, or meaning. In fact, Solomon flatly denies that anyone can discover life's purpose on the basis of empirical observation: "Who knows what is good for a person in life, during the few and meaningless days they pass through like a shadow?" (6:12).

Once, as we were studying Hume's guillotine, one of my students cried out, "But there *are* facts about morality in this world. It's a fact that rape is wrong, that racism is wrong."

Another student rebutted, "But those aren't facts like other facts. You can't measure them, see them, weigh them, observe them. They can't be accounted for in any material way."

And the first student quickly responded to her, "Well, then how do you know they exist?"

And then the whole class together got to observe the look on the first student's face when it dawned on him that he had answered his own question. We *don't* know that they exist, not like scientifically observable facts. They are not facts that are either true or false. They are directions on how one *ought* to live. For moral truths like, "This is how we ought to live," to be true, the answers will have to come from outside of scientific observation. Solomon knew that he needed to be more than a scientist in order to find moral or transcendent meaning, in order to say, "This is how you ought to live."

THE MORE KNOWLEDGE, THE MORE GRIEF

With much wisdom comes much sorrow;
the more knowledge, the more grief.[23]

The second reason "under the sun" wisdom cannot lead to a meaningful life is because the more you know and the more you relate the things you know to a life "under the sun" (without reference to a transcendent metanarrative), the more painful life becomes. This is simple fact. Consider the adage "ignorance is bliss."

Philosopher Joel Marks, in an essay titled "Ignorance Is Bliss," works through some of these ideas. As a philosopher who can't stop asking questions and gathering data about *everything,* he finds himself obsessing over facts about marriage, since he's about to start his second. And the facts aren't promising: Most marriages end in divorce, and *second* marriages are 72 percent likely to end in divorce. His thoughts on the matter? "Just as I know that someday I am going to die, I know that this marriage is likely to fail. . . . It is little comfort to know that one is likely doomed no matter what."[24] Ignorance is bliss. If he knew less about the realities of marriage, he might be able to start his second one with some hope. But he simply can't, knowing it's irrational to believe it'll work out. The odds are stacked against his marriage.

And so there is something both the person who believes that God gives the world cosmic meaning and the atheist who believes this world has no cosmic meaning can agree on: this world can be a miserable place. The more one is either gathering statistics like Marks or simply watching the news (and in a sense soaking in the "under the sun" knowledge of what's going on in this world), the more one learns of the massive suffering throughout the world— everything from the evils of terrorism and political troubles to natural disasters and calamities to the unlikelihood of happily ever after. To learn about this world is essentially to grow in the knowledge of things that can grieve us. As writer Ta-Nehisi Coates observes autobiographically, "It began to strike me that the point of my education was a kind of discomfort . . . and would leave me only with humanity in all its terribleness."[25]

Just this past week, in my vocation as pastor, I counseled two different men grieving over two different close friends who were dying of cancer and whose deaths were imminent. I prayed with a South Sudanese refugee who, having been separated from his nephew during a violent attack, didn't know where in the world his nephew could be found. I set up an appointment with a young man who had written to me in an email, "We need to talk. I can't live like this anymore. I need help." I encouraged one young lady struggling with an unplanned pregnancy. I contacted a pastor about a Muslim convert to Christianity whom I was sending his way—a convert that couldn't go back home for fear of death. And that's only this past week, and only what I can remember off the top of my head. The more you get to know people, the more you learn about this world—and so the more you learn about the rampant injustice, pain, and suffering.

We mentioned earlier in our comparison of the fantasy writers Tolkien and Martin that the world is full of injustice, pain, and suffering. The only question is whether the injustice, pain, and suffering are part of a much larger story that will end well (a knowledge that cannot be discovered "under the sun") or whether the injustice, pain, and suffering are purposeless by-products of a cosmically meaningless existence. Both believer and unbeliever alike may hope that the more we learn, the more we'll be able to help people, and that's true, but with increased knowledge to help simply comes increased knowledge of our inability to help with certain things as well. So this pursuit of knowledge, Solomon declares, is "a chasing after the wind." It's an attempt to achieve something unattainable, something that continues to remain forever outside our grasp.

Of course, what's *not* outside our grasp is to help *some* people. And we can think of times a single individual was able to help lots of people in significant ways. (Insert your favorite humanitarian, inventor, or activist here.) Tyson is right that progress can in some sense be made: "When a problem arises that needs a solution, you will say, 'I know how to solve that; I've been thinking about that before.'" By all means, work hard at finding cures and helpful inventions and useful discoveries. I was recently watching videos of color-blind people being given glasses that could allow them to see color. It's clear that knowledge can lead to tremendous good and aid in overall well-being, allowing people literally to see life better! But despite the good that can be done, the evils seem to multiply just as quickly. For every discovery used for good, someone finds a way to use it for evil. And the more you grow in your ability to help people, the more people you find who need help.

The theologian Martin Luther wrote about this topic this way:

> **Anyone who sees much and knows how it is to go cannot help becoming angry. He thinks: Oh, how miserably and dreadfully things happen in this world! What is the source of this anger and indignation except much wisdom? For anyone who is very wise has many reasons to become angry, as one who daily sees many things that are wrong.**[26]

This is the second reason "under the sun" wisdom cannot lead to a meaningful life: without a metanarrative to put the sufferings and injustices of this life into context, the pursuit of knowledge leads to an endless, weary journey of trying to straighten out something that's hopelessly crooked.

THE SAME FATE OVERTAKES BOTH THE WISE AND THE FOOLISH

Solomon states clearly our third reason why striving after "under the sun" wisdom leads only to frustration. He writes:

> I saw that wisdom is better than folly,
>   just as light is better than darkness.
> The wise have eyes in their heads,
>   while the fool walks in the darkness;
> but I came to realize
>   that the same fate overtakes them both.

Then I said to myself,
  "The fate of the fool will overtake me also.
  What then do I gain by being wise?" . . .
I said to myself,
  "This too is meaningless."
For the wise, like the fool, will not be long remembered;
  the days have already come when both
    have been forgotten.
Like the fool, the wise too must die! (Ecclesiastes 2:13-16)

Solomon's observations here are a variation of a major theme of Ecclesiastes that we'll explore in greater depth in chapter 4, "Work Is Meaningless." This major theme involves the juxtaposition of striving after accomplishment and the inevitability of death. Whereas a businessperson might strive to amass a financial empire or a politician a civic empire, scholars and scientists at times strive after their own empire-building, building the kingdom of knowledge. Remember Tyson's words: "And so when I think of meaning in life, I ask, 'Am I learning something today that I didn't know yesterday?' bringing me a little closer to knowing all that can be known in the universe." Intellectuals can turn knowledge into a goal as much as anything else.

But remember our city of Atlantis? Imagine now that there is a group of scientists in Atlantis that achieves the ultimate scientific goal, what Tyson himself stated as the goal of "knowing all that can be known in the universe." Not one fact or another but *all* the facts—the triumph of the empirical sciences. (Throw in whatever is necessary to make this the ultimate intellectual triumph: the theory of everything, a complete catalog of all living things, a total mastery of genetics, etc.) But then Atlantis sinks, along with all the scientists and their libraries—their knowledge totally lost, never to be seen again. And the world turns as if Atlantis and its triumph of the empirical sciences had never been.

Again, from a cosmic point of view, if this universe is all there is, Atlantis' scientific triumph would be nothing more than a blip in the timeline of the cosmos. Certainly we could talk of there being short-term meaning generated during the existence of Atlantis, but not cosmic. Nothing of lasting value would have been accomplished, and so nothing of cosmic value. What this demonstrates is that the amassing of knowledge *in and of itself* generates no cosmic meaning. If the atheists are right that there is no rhyme or reason to this universe and it simply stretches on into infinite, a time will come for *every* scientist and learned person when their work is utterly forgotten (along with its effects). It will not matter one whit whether they existed and discovered the things they did. In this sense, Solomon declares, "The wise, like the fool, will not be long remembered; the days have already come when both have been forgotten." Ultimately, "the same fate overtakes them both," and this makes wisdom truly meaningless.

Solomon expresses this in his own parable found further within Ecclesiastes:

> I also saw under the sun this example of wisdom that greatly impressed me: There was once a small city with only a few people in it. And a powerful king came against it, surrounded it and built huge siege works against it. Now there lived in that city a man poor but wise, and he saved the city by his wisdom. But nobody remembered that poor man. So I said, "Wisdom is better than strength." But the poor man's wisdom is despised, and his words are no longer heeded. (Ecclesiastes 9:13-16)

Time and death march on, blotting out every memory of ingenuity, every dissertation, every wiki-page. Thus, we have our final reason why the pursuit of knowledge "under the sun," that is, the pursuit of knowledge in and of itself, cannot lead to the cosmically meaningful life.

WHO KNOWS? I KNOW

We know so little about this world. A friend told me about a debate he had attended between a Christian and an atheist on whether or not God existed. After the atheist had given his 15-minute opener, the Christian apologist stepped forward and said, "I'm just going to need a minute of your time." On a giant pad of paper, he drew a circle, and he said, "Imagine inside of this circle is all the knowledge about our universe. How much do you think we know?" He then drew a single dot within the circle. "Maybe about that much?" The audience murmured in agreement. "So, you're telling me that based on this much knowledge," he said, pointing at the dot, "you can be certain that in the rest of this," he gestured at the rest of the circle, "there are no good reasons to believe in God?" Maybe you don't think this is a very valid line of reasoning for defending belief in God, but when my friend told me this story, the circle and the dot stuck with me. It's true. Based on everything that *could* be known, we know very little.

Solomon knows he doesn't know a lot. Despite dedicating so much of his life to the pursuit of knowledge, he says over and over, "Who knows?"

> *Who knows* whether that person will be wise or foolish? Yet they will have control over all the fruit of my toil into which I have poured my effort and skill under the sun. (Ecclesiastes 2:19)

> *Who knows* if the human spirit rises upward and if the spirit of the animal goes down into the earth? (Ecclesiastes 3:21)

> *Who knows* what is good for a person in life, during the few and meaningless days they pass through like a shadow? (Ecclesiastes 6:12)

> Whatever exists is far off and most profound—*who* can discover it? (Ecclesiastes 7:24)

Solomon utters the phrase "who knows" almost always in the midst of his meditations on life "under the sun," on the apparent meaninglessness and randomness of life. Assessing what we can learn about our universe "under the sun" simply through the gathering of empirical data and experiences is a humbling experience.

But there are moments, albeit fleeting and few, when Solomon says that he *does know*. For example, at one point he writes:

> **What do workers gain from their toil? I have seen the burden God has laid on the human race. He has made everything beautiful in its time. He has also set eternity in the human heart; yet no one can fathom what God has done from beginning to end. *I know* that there is nothing better for people than to be happy and to do good while they live. That each of them may eat and drink, and find satisfaction in all their toil—this is the gift of God. *I know* that everything God does will endure forever; nothing can be added to it and nothing taken from it. God does it so that people will fear him. (Ecclesiastes 3:9-14)**

Solomon knows several things about God. He knows:

- God has made everything beautiful in its time.

- God has set eternity in the human heart.

- God's own knowledge about the future is unfathomable/ unknowable.

- God has given us the gift of being able to enjoy food and drink and work.

- God's works endure forever.

- God desires people to fear him. (Again, *fear* means "a childlike mingling of awe, love, trust, and healthy fearful recognition for God's might and strength.")

Is this Solomon letting his faith interrupt his cynicism? Or is it possible that this is all stuff that one can know "under the sun"? Not only Christians but followers of almost *every* religion throughout history believe that if there is a God (or gods), these are the types of attributes he would have. If there is a God that has created this universe, he has made it so that the seasons bring about beauty and life regularly, he has placed a striving for eternity and spiritual things in the hearts of people, he and his knowledge are beyond us, etc.

Either way, here are important things to know, important things that can be known arguably outside the scope or reach of observational, empirical science. Going back to the big circle with the small dot inside, a worldview that limits itself to empirical science isn't even looking at the whole dot. Nor is it using its whole heart.

THE MEANINGFUL PURSUIT OF KNOWLEDGE, OR THE SCIENTIFIC CHRISTIAN

It ought to be clear by now that the scientific pursuit of knowledge promoted by Tyson cannot actually deliver a life of cosmic (or moral) meaning. Again, scientists and academics do plenty of meaningful work understood in a short-term sense. Theoretical physicist Jim Al-Khalili, a popularizer of science and a sort of British version of the American Tyson, observes:

> If you trace back all those links in the chain that had to be in place for me to be here, the laws of probability maintain that my very existence is miraculous. But then after however many decades, less than a hundred years, they disperse and I cease to be. So while they're all congregated and coordinated to make me, . . . I should really make the most of things.[27]

And he's right. It's commendable to make the most of things. But the fact is that not only people but *everything* will disperse and cease to be. And with everything else, the short-term meaning derived from our pursuit of wisdom will cease. If we want to give the pursuit of wisdom its most meaningful context, one in which its pursuit *does*, in fact, contribute to cosmic meaning, it must first be understood within the biblical metanarrative.

Was the Bible meant to address questions of science at all? The great African theologian Saint Augustine of Hippo argued (in a debate in A.D. 392) that Jesus did not send the Holy Spirit to his church to "'teach you about the course of the sun and the moon'; for he wanted to make Christians, not mathematicians."[28] Plenty of people today think that science and the belief that God created and rules over everything are two mutually exclusive positions. And I would concede that some fields of science raise head-scratching questions on how to fit what we observe in the world with the biblical accounts of God creating it all. But in many other ways, the biblical narrative fits squarely within how a scientist understands the world. Most important, it satisfies science-lovers' deep longing for their scientific discoveries to have cosmic, moral, and lasting meaning.

In fact, the first few chapters of the Bible directly address this. The book of Genesis opens with the words, "In the beginning God created the heavens and the earth." We learn immediately that there is a mind behind our universe. After this follows a beautiful description of this orderly and rational God creating a world of order and rationality, where even the most massive astronomical objects serve to mark the seasons and time in an orderly way and where even the most exotic specimens of this world's biodiversity reproduce in an orderly way. We might be tempted to gloss over that repeated phrase, that the living things produce "according to their kinds," not realizing the enormous weight of those words: God has given us a world in which we ought to *expect* and *anticipate* patterns, arrangement, and design. In other words, God has given us a world in which we can do science, a world in which artists can find rhythm and regularity, a world that can be explored. And then God created the scientists, artists, and explorers for this world. The next chapter of Genesis even tells us that God created humans to live within this world as its ultimate caretakers. This is the metanarrative Solomon believes we ought to rightly understand wisdom within when he writes, "Remember your Creator" (Ecclesiastes 12:1—see also 7:29 and 12:7).

When a scientist understands her vocation within this metanarrative—that God created a world perfect for doing science and then created people with the capacity to do science—then the scientist sees herself as doing *what she was created to do*. God expects all of his creatures to learn about his creation in some capacity, and he has clearly gifted some with the desire and the skills to do it professionally (such as Solomon himself!).

But it is not only the Creator's orderliness that gives meaning and metanarrative to our scientific pursuits but even more so his character. The Jewish novelist and Nobel laureate Isaac Bashevis Singer wrote about this contrast between Genesis' metanarrative and secularized science's lack thereof:

> My father and mother always told me that God was a god of justice, on the side of the weak, not only the strong. But I heard my [atheist] brother remark that nature does not know any compassion; it acts according to eternal laws. He quoted the great Jewish philosopher Benedict de Spinoza, who said that we must love nature with an intellectual love. But how can we love something or someone who knows no pity and perhaps does not love us? . . .

> In my years of literary growth, I had a chance to read Homer's *Iliad* and *Odyssey*. His style was perfect but soulless. Homer's protagonists were wild, cruel, half mad, without any feeling for right and wrong, without any compassion for human life. Their gods were as savage as they themselves. The god of [the book of Genesis] fills the human heart with hope, and gives meaning to our joys and to our sorrows. What is true about Homer can also be said about the scientists of his time, and even those in our time. There is little comfort in the science of today and in its cosmology. It has filled the universe with idols we can never love or even respect. Only the most insensitive can accept the notion that the universe is a

result of a cosmic bomb which exploded some twenty billion years ago and continues to run away from itself forever.

No matter how the human brain might grow, it will always come back to the idea that God has created heaven and earth, man and animals, with a will and a plan, and that, despite all the evil life undergoes, there is a purpose in Creation and eternal wisdom.[29]

The first two chapters of Genesis give us more than a God of order. This Creator did more than simply create a complex, yet ordered and principled, world. He created people. *Other* people. People he wanted to be with. He wanted a world of not only organisms but families and relationships. And he wanted them to be in *his* family; he wanted to walk with them, talk with them, care for them along the riverbanks of their botanical and zoological paradise. This God loves to shelter, to preserve, to empower, to give what is good.

Knowing this God gives meaning to science, its applications, and its wisdom. This wisdom, Solomon says, is indeed "a good thing and benefits those who see the sun" (Ecclesiastes 7:11). It "is a shelter" and "preserves those who have it" (7:12). It makes a person "more powerful than ten rulers" (7:19) and "is better than weapons of war" (9:18). When the scientist combines the intellectual accomplishments of her mind with a hopeful and joyous heart—a heart that desires to shelter, preserve, empower; a heart that desires to heal, make flourish, create, and strengthen relationships—she can be assured that she does what God loves. She restores her little corner of this spoiled world more to what God made it to be. She gives his love a face and hands.

———————————— • ————————————

THREE

PLEASURES ARE

MEANINGLESS

———•———

THE NEW RICH

I had stretched myself too thin. I had said *yes* to too many projects, boards, committees, and task forces. Between my family, the church family I served as a pastor, and the invitations to help the Christian church on a larger scale, I just simply didn't have enough time. I couldn't get it all done. Something had to give. At least one of my major commitments had to be broken. But how would I choose?

One of my closest friends said, "Well, obviously not family or church, so what can you say no to on the larger scale?"

I explained they were all pretty important.

"Well, then which one makes you *least* happy? Which ones aren't you getting much enjoyment out of?"

You mean I can make the choice based simply on *what makes me most happy?*

Obviously, we all want to be happy, but how much *should* the pursuit of happiness play into our lives? How much attention should personal happiness get? To what degree should personal pleasures in life sway decision-making? And, by the way, finishing this book was on the list. How much should concern for my own personal happiness have determined whether you ever read this?

There's an interesting movement afoot among middle to upper-middle class Gen Xers and millennials called the *New Rich* (not to be confused with the largely derogatory phrase *nouveau riche*). Whereas past generations saw the goal of life as amassing wealth doing whatever work was necessary (including work you didn't really enjoy) to secure a comfy retirement, the New Rich suggest that's getting things backwards. Why spend your best days doing work that's often unfulfilling or not enjoyable so that when you begin to slow down and have aches and pains, *then* you get to enjoy yourself? That paradigm should be turned on its head! The goal *ought to be* to design a life in which you can enjoy yourself now! There are two strategies for doing this: (1) Work more efficiently and in bursts of greater intensity, with the goal of then being able to take frequent extended breaks (e.g., work like a dog for six months and then take six months off traveling the world or work like a dog for nine months and then take three incredible months hiking the Andes). (2) Maximize the aspects of your work you enjoy and minimize (via delegation, etc.) the parts of your work you don't like.

In Timothy Ferriss' *The 4-Hour Workweek*, one of the bibles of the New Rich movement, Ferriss explains:

> Most people, my past self included, have spent too much time convincing themselves that life has to be hard, a resignation to 9-to-5 drudgery in exchange for (sometimes) relaxing weekends and the occasional keep-it-short-or-get-fired vacation. The truth, at least the truth I live and will share in this book, is quite different. From leveraging currency differences to outsourcing your life and disappearing, I'll show you how a small underground uses economic sleight-of-hand to do what most consider impossible.[30]

This is no gimmick. Ferriss certainly does teach the skills to live a New Rich lifestyle, which many Westerners today are finding themselves able to achieve. And let's be clear: There's nothing wrong with applying Ferriss' strategies to one's life or even adopting a New Rich mind-set for how you might design your life. What might be interesting, though, is pausing for a moment and asking, But what's the motivation? For Timothy Ferriss, at the end of *The 4-Hour Workweek*, he tells us clearly, "I believe that life exists to be enjoyed." (Not too far removed from the Dalai Lama: "The purpose of our lives is to be happy.")

Slow down for a minute and think about that: "Life exists to be enjoyed." Notice how Ferriss taps into the concepts we've been discussing. By saying, "Life *exists to be . . . ,*" he's saying there's a purpose to life. And by now we've seen that there's a limited number of ways this might be the case: either there's a cosmic purpose, that is, the universe exists or has been brought into existence for at least one purpose, perhaps that humans (or other self-reflective creatures) enjoy themselves; or there's moral meaning in life and a person is living the correct way if they're striving to enjoy themselves and not living the correct way if they're *not* striving to enjoy themselves. (And remember that moral meaning can only be derived from a universe with cosmic meaning, so the two are definitely related.)

Ferriss and other New Rich advocates would certainly agree that you can define *enjoyment* in many different, acceptable ways— from the adrenaline rush of extreme adventures like hang gliding to the sense of fulfillment that comes from helping those in need. (And, in fact, Ferriss would probably agree with the studies that say life's greatest happiness is generated by helping others rather than self pleasure or gratification.) So he's not a straight-up hedonist. (We'll define that later.) But regardless of how one generates these feelings of enjoyment, the end goal is still what we might call a *life of pleasure* (pleasure being understood broadly, not just as physical pleasure but also fulfillment, etc.) or a life of accumulating pleasurable experiences. And if this isn't just Ferriss' view, but if he's tapping into a more widely felt vibe in Western culture, no wonder we take so many selfies! We're storing up so many of these experiences because we depend on them for our meaning in life!

But is it true that you *should* be pursuing a life of happiness? Should this really be the sum total of your goals in life? Is this really all there is to it? And if so, what happens if you fail to experience happiness? Have you failed at life? Or here's the bigger question: If you're looking for a cosmically meaningful life, a life that is important and valuable *not just because you value it* but because it actually *is* valuable, can this be achieved through pursuing a life of pleasure and happiness? Believing that the purpose of life is to be happy is far more complicated than it looks. And this is one of the reasons why, even three thousand years ago, Solomon touches upon it. Did Solomon find a life of pursuing pleasures any more fulfilling and meaningful than a life of pursuing science and learning?

SOLOMON RICH

If anyone had a lifestyle that afforded him every pleasure, it was Solomon. Solomon's reign was reputed to have been a golden age of prosperity for Israel. The book of the Bible titled 1 Kings, which records Solomon's life, tells us, "The people of Judah and Israel were as numerous as the sand on the seashore; they ate, they drank and they were happy" (1 Kings 4:20). "The king made silver as common in Jerusalem as stones" (1 Kings 10:27). Besides ruling with great wisdom and judgment, Solomon generated a tremendous amount of wealth for Israel, overseeing the construction of architectural monoliths, such as what we call the temple of Solomon (one of the great wonders of the ancient world). His reputation spread to distant nations. Consider the following account of the famous visit of the queen of Sheba:

> When the queen of Sheba heard about the fame of Solomon and his relationship to the LORD, she came to test Solomon with hard questions. Arriving at Jerusalem with a very great

caravan—with camels carrying spices, large quantities of gold, and precious stones—she came to Solomon and talked with him about all that she had on her mind. Solomon answered all her questions; nothing was too hard for the king to explain to her. When the queen of Sheba saw all the wisdom of Solomon and the palace he had built, the food on his table, the seating of his officials, the attending servants in their robes, his cupbearers, and the burnt offerings he made at the temple of the LORD, she was overwhelmed.

She said to the king, "The report I heard in my own country about your achievements and your wisdom is true. But I did not believe these things until I came and saw with my own eyes. Indeed, not even half was told me; in wisdom and wealth you have far exceeded the report I heard. How happy your people must be! How happy your officials, who continually stand before you and hear your wisdom! Praise be to the LORD your God, who has delighted in you and placed you on the throne of Israel. Because of the LORD's eternal love for Israel, he has made you king to maintain justice and righteousness." . . .

King Solomon gave the queen of Sheba all she desired and asked for, besides what he had given her out of his royal bounty. Then she left and returned with her retinue to her own country. (1 Kings 10:1-13)

Solomon goes down as one of the richest men recorded in the Bible, getting everything his heart desired. Sometimes his heart desired good things; sometimes, questionable things (such as his hundreds of slave-wives, his trade in exotic animals and ivory, and his extensive customer list as an international arms dealer). And sometimes his riches were the result of other people's labors. (He famously conscripted tens of thousands of forced laborers for his great architectural projects.) Regardless, though, if one could generate a meaningful life from pleasures, surely Solomon was the man to give it a try: he had the brains and money to do it, for sure. Yet this is how he responds at the end of his life to a life of generating so much pleasure:

> I said to myself, "Come now, I will test you with pleasure to find out what is good." But that also proved to be meaningless. "Laughter," I said, "is madness. And what does pleasure accomplish?" I tried cheering myself with wine, and embracing folly—my mind still guiding me with wisdom. I wanted to see what was good for people to do under the heavens during the few days of their lives.
>
> I undertook great projects: I built houses for myself and planted vineyards. I made gardens and parks and planted all kinds of fruit trees in them. I made reservoirs to water groves of flourishing trees. I bought male and female slaves and had other slaves who were born in my house. I also owned more herds and flocks than anyone in Jerusalem before me. I amassed silver and gold for myself, and the treasure of kings and provinces. I acquired male and female singers, and a harem as well—the delights of a man's heart. I became greater by far than anyone in Jerusalem before me. In all this my wisdom stayed with me.
>
> I denied myself nothing my eyes desired;
>   I refused my heart no pleasure.
> My heart took delight in all my labor,
>   and this was the reward for all my toil.
> Yet when I surveyed all that my hands had done
>   and what I had toiled to achieve,
> everything was meaningless, a chasing after the wind;
>   nothing was gained under the sun. (Ecclesiastes 2:1-11)

Literary critic and former *The New Yorker* editor Daphne Merkin describes Solomon as an "acquisition-happy malcontent, this Biblical character blessed with the dazzling 'life style' of a corporate raider but burdened with the wrong soul." What happened? How could Solomon have achieved so many pleasures and yet feel so empty? How can having so much be so meaningless? We live in a culture that places the pursuit of wealth and pleasurable experiences as one of the highest goals in life. Think of everything we've been taught to pursue! Whether termed as financial security or contentment or straight-up physical gratification, it's really largely about happiness. How could so many people be so wrong? How is this all "a chasing after the wind"? How is it possible that, after a New Rich life of accumulated experiences, Solomon would say "nothing was gained"?

HEDONISM

For millennia, philosophers and thinkers have struggled with understanding what role happiness plays in pursuing a meaningful life. In fact, thousands of years ago, there was a school of philosophy that focused on creating lives built on pleasure. (Its spirit is very much alive in some philosophers today.) The most famous spokesman was Epicurus, who writes:

> **Pleasure is the beginning and end of the blessed life. We recognize pleasure as the first and natural good; starting from pleasure we accept or reject; and we return to this as we judge every good thing, trusting this feeling of pleasure as our guide.[31]**

Epicurus is *not* promoting a life of senseless pleasure-seeking, drugs, uninhibited sex, and watching TV every day. He responds to his critics that pursuing those types of things obviously doesn't lead to a sustainable, deep, pleasurable life. Your life would simply be miserable. Rather, the pleasurable life includes a good amount of moderation—something akin to the wellness movement today that promotes a disciplined life, especially in regards to diet, exercise, mental stimulation, and psychologically healthy habits and thinking (but also being careful not to overspend on vitamins or probiotics).

So, with those caveats in mind, how might we assess Epicurus? You might have many questions for Epicurus: How do you know what will be most pleasurable in the long run? Is Epicurus reducing everything we call ethically *good* to pleasures? If so, aren't there things that are clearly good but do not derive pleasure (such as self-sacrifice)? And aren't there things that are pleasurable, even in the long run, that aren't necessarily good (such as enslaving or harming a small amount of innocent people to bring about long-lasting pleasure for a larger group)? Many philosophers have found Epicurus' raising of one's pleasure as the highest good to be hard if not impossible to harmonize with concepts like human rights, the value of great acts of altruism (such as giving one's life, which doesn't lead to much lasting pleasure for oneself), or the importance of duty. For these reasons and others, not many philosophers today (although there are a few) consider themselves Epicureans.

But there are deeper questions than just these philosophical ones. The Danish Lutheran thinker Soren Kierkegaard once wrote a story with a character that attempted to live his life as a hedonist (and not the moderate type that Epicurus championed; this was a party animal). This aesthete, as Kierkegaard called him, recognized that things are most pleasurable when they are novel (even skydiving might lose its initial rush after the one hundredth jump), and so the best way to live is to forget as much as possible. In this way, one could try to make oneself nothing but a collection of pleasurable experiences. But note what follows:

> **My life is utterly meaningless. When I consider the different periods into which it falls, it seems like the word *Schnur* in the dictionary, which means in the first place a string, in the second, a daughter-in-law. The only thing lacking is that the word *Schnur* should mean in the third place a camel, in the fourth, a dust brush.[32]**

Let's consider Kierkegaard's line of thought with a more familiar word from our own dictionaries. The term *bank* can mean both a riverbank as well as a bank for money (or even the tilt an airplane makes as it turns). The definitions have nothing in common at all, only that they coincidentally share the same word to designate those definitions. A person defining her life in terms of pleasures and nothing else is similar—while every moment might be unique for that person, there's no real relationship to tie one pleasurable experience to the next except that they coincidentally happen to the same person. My friend Topher pointed out that it's as if a person's life was a similar dictionary entry: "**Joe's Life** (n.) 1. He went on a roller coaster once. 2. He got hung over 30 times in college. 3. He was almost brave enough to eat pufferfish." There is no thread to tie one's life experiences together, and so you really can't think of yourself as having any real robust identity.

Kierkegaard's whole point is that life becomes meaningless if we define our lives entirely by the events that make them up, striving to make each event as pleasurable as possible and to escape boredom with as much variety as possible. With no metanarrative running through the events of our lives, there is no essence or personal identity to recognize, just a creature experiencing event after event. If you define your meaning in life through the pleasurable experiences you are collecting, take away the events and you're left with nothing.

We can understand intuitively enough that the simple activity of collecting *things* won't deliver a cosmically meaningful life. It can bring a level of pleasure to be sure, and it generates short-term meaning to be sure. But transient stuff, here today and gone tomorrow, lacks permanence. And treating experiences like things that can be collected can produce the same results. This would explain your feeling when you look back at your life as simply a collection of self-serving events. When you consider these events "under the sun" apart from the biblical metanarrative, life really is cosmically meaningless. There's nothing you can consider that ties things together into something coherent, permanent, or of lasting value.

And this goes either for Epicurus' moderate hedonism or a more radical version. Even if the life you're pursuing is one of healthy, well-balanced, carefully budgeted pleasures and experiences—like the pleasurable sensations of a fit, flexible, yoga-toned body; the rush of reaching a mountain peak; or the pleasure of creating a work of art—the same problems exist for you as they do for the person pursuing a life of not-so-healthy pleasures and experiences—like endless Netflix binges, street racing, or living for the next Friday night orgy. At the end of the day, for cosmic meaning, these experiences need to be anchored in a greater overarching story that gives them *real* significance. Otherwise, these are just simply *events,* pleasures that will one day be forgotten and inconsequential.

THE FEW DAYS OF OUR LIVES

In fact, focusing on how many pleasurable experiences we can generate out of life can become a tremendous source of angst, a midlife crisis that's available to us at any moment of our lives. The average lifespan in North America right now is 80 years, or 29,200 days. If we focus on what our culture considers the productive number of days an average person lives (so not counting early life or maybe the last five years), that leaves us with 65 years, or 23,725 days. That's 3,389 weeks and around 780 months. Now think for a moment about how much you've done with your time. Solomon lists his "accomplishments" carried out for the sake of a pleasurable life: building projects, amassing wealth in terms of servants and gold, groves of trees. Today the average middle-class Westerner might compare these to long-term accomplishments, like trying to develop a good career, a fat bank account, successful children, and a nice house and lawn. Like Solomon, we derive as much pleasure as we can out of these things—possessions, wardrobe, cars, financial security, vacations, and experiences—but then at some point we catch ourselves pausing, thinking about all these things and experiences we've collected, and asking ourselves, "But what of real *value* have I done with my life?" You realize you've spent hours upon hours watching

TV, hours upon hours shopping, hours upon hours sleeping, hours upon hours socializing with friends and family (or sitting together just to look at your phones), and all of a sudden half of your life seems to have passed and what do you have to show for it?

We can dig even deeper into the vital soul of the question by understanding it in the context of *good works*. *Good works* is a theological term for describing the things God has created humans to do, that is, the actions that please God when we do them. Christians believe God has put into all people a conscience, which can easily identify some of these things. If you're not a Christian, chances are you still feel like you have a conscience that recognizes some of the same things: helping those in need and putting the necessities of others first, as well as making choices that *avoid* harming others. (This is summed up in the Bible as "love your neighbor as yourself," but it finds its expression in other religions as well, such as Confucius' "do not do to others what you would not want them to do to you.")

And when we compare this to our lives that have spent so much time on *self*-gratification, on serving *my* needs first, despite all of the opportunities to serve others, we start to see a problem: So much of our lives has been spent bypassing good works. So much of our lives has been self-centered, not other-centered; self-serving, not other-serving. We stroll through our homes, looking up and down at the Blu-ray collections, furniture, closets full of clothes, and we begin to feel *guilt*, guilt that we've been seeking to take care of ourselves far more than others.

And it doesn't stop there. Not only do we find ourselves *neglecting* others, but often we're *actively hurting* others. A non-Christian friend of mine named Amber has a brother (also not a Christian) who's really into body modification. Really into it. Face tattoos, eyes dyed black, a dozen piercings on his head, even small implanted horns. All in the name of personal expression. Amber told me—close to tears—about a funeral her brother wasn't allowed to attend because of his appearance. "The priest told him he's not welcome," she said. No follow-up from the priest, no further discussion. And then came the big questions: "Can he do that? Do you ever refuse to let people into a funeral, into a church service?" I told her I didn't want to condemn the priest too hastily, but in general, "No, we don't ever refuse people. If the person is there to listen, the whole church family has an obligation to do everything possible to welcome that person. In fact, that's the one place I'd want your brother, at the funeral, where he might be able to find real comfort in Jesus for that death in his life." It's so easy to judge, to say I'd do better than the priest. We're all awesome at retrospectively figuring out what ought to have been done. And maybe there's more to the story that Amber and I don't know. My only point is this: If Amber's got the story right, her brother wasn't simply neglected, overlooked, forgotten about. He was actively hurt, willfully rejected from a community event, knowingly barred from an event that was designed to give hope in the midst of tragedy. We *know* this happens to people. All the time.

And I know that I also live a life of actively hurting others, as do you: lying, bullying, making fun, telling or laughing at hurtful jokes, objectifying people, persuading people into wrong actions, you name it. So we add this to the list of what defines us and our lives: Our lives are not only about amassing things and pleasures and spending time on ourselves rather than on others but even actively taking the pleasure and happiness *away* from others. If we're honest, the *few days of our lives* have been, in essence, as far as the rest of humanity goes, *wasted*.

But the Teacher clearly expects us *not* to waste our lives through selfishness and acts of injustice. He writes, in fact, that he believes his God takes considerable issue with this. For those who do evil, "there will be . . . a time to judge every deed" (Ecclesiastes 3:17). If there *is* a God, he certainly expects people not to waste their lives on self-directed pleasure-seeking but rather to live a life of serving others. And if we can't do these good works that God requires, and at times even find ourselves *not wanting* to do these good works, why would God want to spend eternity with people who are more interested in themselves than others, people that replace happiness with pain? The only solution is for the Creator to find a way to fix the creation gone wrong, and we're right back at the metanarrative: The Bible promises that God has a good ending in mind, an ending in which this selfishness, pain, and suffering will come to an end.

SURELY THERE'S MORE TO IT

Alvin Plantinga could very well go down in history as one of the greatest philosophers of the turn of the 21st century. With seven honorary degrees and many prestigious academic awards like the Templeton Prize, *Time* magazine has described him as "America's leading orthodox Protestant philosopher." As a Christian spending a lifetime of *thinking* on *how to think* about Christianity, he believes there's still plenty left to do to figure out how the biblical metanarrative sheds light on our deepest longings and experiences as humans. For example, at the end of a festschrift (a collection of essays celebrating his scholarship), he shares the notes to a short talk he gave titled "Two Dozen (or so) Theistic Arguments," the purpose of which was to show young thinkers that there's plenty of room for exploring the implications of the biblical metanarrative in philosophy. One of his arguments for God's existence (here *argument* simply means "a line of reasoning") goes as follows:

The Argument [for God's existence] from Play and Enjoyment:

. . . Evolution [says]: [Play and enjoyment is] an adaptive means of preparing for adult life (so that engaging in this sort of thing as an adult suggests a case of arrested development). But surely there is more to it than that. The joy one can take in humor, art, poetry, mountaineering, exploring, adventuring (the problem is not to explain how it would come about that human beings enjoyed mountaineering: no doubt evolution can do so. The problem is with its significance. Is it really true that all there is to this is enjoyment? Or is there

a deeper significance? The Westminster Shorter Catechism [says]: the chief end of man is to glorify God and enjoy him (and his creation and gifts) forever).[33]

Do you follow Plantinga? Sophisticated atheistic evolutionary explanations certainly can be made for how play, pleasure, and enjoyment have come to be part of the human experience in all cultures. We can see how evolving the capacity to experience enjoyment might motivate the learning of certain skills that help a species survive. For example, puppies "play fight" with each other and in doing so learn how to really fight. But if that's the only reason we give for why humans enjoy things (it benefits their survival), something seems to be lacking. "Surely there is more to it than that," Plantinga says. Do humans *enjoy* companionship only because it's useful for the survival of the species, or is there more to it than that? Do humans *take pleasure* in a sunset only because it's somehow useful for the survival of the species, or is there more to it than that? Do humans *seek adventure* only because it's somehow useful for the survival of the species, or is there more to it than that? If that is all there is to it, then that means there's nothing inherently good about companionship, sunsets, or adventures. Instead, it would seem that the idea that sunsets are good arises from within *us*—the feeling that they're good simply being a feeling placed there to help us survive. Given atheistic evolution, sunsets simply *are;* they are simply another thing within this universe that came into existence through random forces. But something deep within us tells us that there *is* something inherently good about these things. That whether or not people are around to find sunsets beautiful (or anyone cares enough to notice sunsets anymore), they still *are* beautiful.

And when we feel pleasure in other things, such as gossiping, hurting other people, and getting away with crimes, can we justify these feelings of pleasure at least in part (or at least in the past) as somehow useful for the survival of our species? Or is there more? Can we say that there's something inherently *bad* about these things?

If we're looking for atheism to give some type of transcendent, cosmic meaning to these actions, we're not going to find it. It's impossible. Atheistic evolutionary explanations can only reduce the meaning to something short-term—something assigned value only for a given time by the sentient creatures involved. But given the Christian metanarrative, things change. All of a sudden it all takes on *epic* meaning. . . .

BUILT FOR PLEASURE

The Christian metanarrative says, "You are right to feel absolutely disappointed in atheistic evolution's explanation for the human experience of pleasure and happiness. The truth is much better, much more in tune with our intuitions. You enjoy and derive pleasure from relationships, sunsets, and adventure because you were literally *designed* to recognize the very real goodness in these things."

Remember our review of the first couple chapters of Genesis? Again recall that the Christian metanarrative begins with God creating humans as scientists and creating the world as a perfect playground where they could discover, research, and do experiments. Similarly God created this world to be *enjoyed*. God created *two* humans, not just one, a husband and a wife, perfect companions so that they could enjoy each other. God said, "It is not good for the man to be alone," and then he created woman (Genesis 2:18). According to the Bible, the first poem in history, and also the first recorded words spoken by a human, was a love poem that praised God for creating a perfect companion and praised God that the two of them were made from the very same substance and essence: "This is now bone of my bones and flesh of my flesh" (Genesis 2:23). God created them with the capacity to bear children, to create families and communities, so that we could have dinners, dates, parties, game nights, pickup basketball, and dances. Some lines from another poem in the Bible celebrate God creating "wine that gladdens human hearts, oil to make their faces shine, and bread that sustains their hearts"

(Psalm 104:15). Jesus himself was criticized by the puritanical for enjoying the camaraderie and dinner parties of hedonists and pleasure-seekers. Speaking of himself, he said, "The Son of Man came eating and drinking, and you say, 'Here is a glutton and a drunkard, a friend of tax collectors and sinners'" (Luke 7:34). We were literally made to be social creatures, deriving pleasure from spending time together, and those pleasurable times together are a *gift from God*. In Solomon's own words, "When God gives someone wealth and possessions, and the ability to enjoy them, . . . this is a *gift of God*" (Ecclesiastes 5:19).

God created humans with an aesthetic sense and placed them within an aesthetically beautiful world. As functional as this world is (the earth rotates while revolving around the sun to give us temperature regulation and seasons), it's also beautiful (the earth rotates to give us sunsets and revolves around the sun to give us summers to swim in lakes and winters to ice skate). And humans have the ability not only to discover and utilize its functionality but also to sit back and take pleasure in its aesthetic beauty, even mirroring and reconfiguring its beauty in works of art. The Canadian poet Marjorie Pickthall believed the aesthetic experience plays such a central role in explaining why God created us that she goes so far as to personify Beauty in the Garden of Eden in one of her brilliant poems, titled "Adam and Eve":

When the first dark had fallen around them
And the leaves were weary of praise,
In the clear silence Beauty found them
And shewed them all her ways.

In the high noon of the heavenly garden
Where the angels sunned with the birds,
Beauty, before their hearts could harden,
Had taught them heavenly words.

God endowed humans with a sense of adventure. Again, there is a functional quality to the hills, streams, oceans, and valleys. And humans were created with the capacity to discover many practical and pragmatic purposes for them and even to take delight in learning those purposes, as another poem in the Bible sings, "Great are the works of the Lord; they are pondered by all who delight in them" (Psalm 111:2). But God also created humans with the desire to hike those hills, canoe those streams, surf and sail those oceans, and hang glide over those valleys. The adrenaline rush feels good, because we were *made* for it to feel good. God wants us to enjoy his creation, revel in it together, and praise his handiwork. In the words of the Christian runner in the movie *Chariots of Fire*, "God made me for a purpose, . . . but he also made me fast. And when I run, I feel his pleasure."

If there's a reason, a design, a purpose for the human ability to enjoy relationships, to take pleasure in sunsets, and to seek the thrill of adventure, and if that purpose comes from above humans themselves and is in fact infused into the very purpose of this universe, then we can say the pleasures we experience are cosmically meaningful. But only if their purpose comes from *over the sun*, as it were. "Under the sun," pleasures considered only within the realms of a godless, purposeless world lose their cosmic meaning.

LIFE WITHOUT PLEASURE

And what of the times life isn't pleasurable? The congregation members I serve in Ottawa, Ontario, work closely with refugees of the Nuer tribe of the South Sudan, and many congregation members have become their close friends. Recently one of these friends, Robert, told me his story. After sharing with me his own life full of warfare, famine, and hardships, he told me that one year ago his brother was killed in the midst of the violence of South Sudan's civil war. His brother's children are now missing, and he's working through all the needed paperwork to travel back to South Sudan to try to find them. He has no idea where they could be or where to start looking.

There is pleasure in this world, and yet there is a good deal of pain. How can we explain these two realities simply by looking around "under the sun"? Solomon himself writes that too often for humankind, "All their days their work is grief and pain; even at night their minds do not rest" (Ecclesiastes 2:23). And, "As fish are caught in a cruel net, or birds are taken in a snare, so people are trapped by evil times that fall unexpectedly upon them" (Ecclesiastes 9:12). What went wrong?

Given a purely empirical or atheistic evolutionary interpretation of experience, there *is* no explanation except to say that pleasure and pain just *are:* they are random results of the chaotic forces of time. Perhaps an ethic of some sort or an explanation for human behavior can be built upon the biological experiences of pursuing pleasure and avoiding pain (what the psychoanalyst Sigmund Freud called *the pleasure principle*). But the resulting portrait of human life is cold, devoid of color and life. The science fiction writer Robert Heinlein, in his Nebula award-winning novel *Starship Troopers*, imagines a future society built on these very principles—one of its ethics professors, also a military instructor, summarizing its ethical foundation:

> Man is what he is, a wild animal with the will to survive, and (so far) the ability against all competition. Unless one accepts that, anything one says about morals, war, politics—you name it—is nonsense. Correct morals arise from knowing what Man is—not what do-gooders and well-meaning old Aunt Nellies would like him to be.

And it can be so appealing to buy into this worldview, because we *do* act like wild animals! But given a Christian metanarrative, although we might act like wild animals at times, we are not simply wild animals. Much of the pain in the world arises not from animal instinct but from all-too-human cruelty, following suit with our first parents following after the Enemy.

The biblical metanarrative puts us in the midst of an epic Story, the greatest tragedy of which is that humans, first through greed (a close cousin of cruelty), walked away from God. In response to this tragedy, God did two nearly incomprehensible things. He promised that someday he would come to earth himself to defeat the Murderer (and be deeply wounded by him). And he also allowed pain and frustration to make its way through our world, so we would never fool ourselves into thinking that we're all right without him. As C. S. Lewis once said, pain is God's "megaphone to rouse a deaf world."

Yes, there still is pleasure in the world, because God limits the Murderer's efforts to destroy *all* that is good—and because, out of love, God still just simply enjoys giving people happiness, even people who treat him like a stranger. But we simply can't derive pleasure from the world as we were first meant to.

Although our hearts yearn for companionship, we never find it perfectly. In fact, sinful humans often recoil from one another—companions even hurting each other, hearts even breaking. Although the occasional sunset still moves us to revel in its beauty, we also see ugliness all around us (and our aesthetic sense is tuned into recognizing ugliness just as much as beauty). Although we desire adventure, life usually feels drab, and adventures end in terror and sadness as much as thrill. God wants us to see that something is lacking in relationships, sunsets, and adventures. There's an ultimate emptiness to it all, until that emptiness is filled with his love. This is why he lets us bear the marks of sin in our souls and in the soil.

The Teacher very much believed in this part of the biblical metanarrative. "What a heavy burden God has laid on mankind!" he laments (Ecclesiastes 1:13). Before the Teacher spends the rest of his scroll describing this heavy burden, he wants you to know that it came from God. Later he writes, "Consider what God has done: Who can straighten what he has made crooked? When times are good, be happy; but when times are bad, consider this: God has made the one as well as the other" (7:13,14). Why are there bad times, painful days? God made them, Solomon says, and no one can unmake them. And again, "When I applied my mind to know wisdom and to observe the labor that is done on earth—people getting no sleep day or night—then I saw all that God has done" (8:16,17). And so the Christian (and the Teacher's) metanarrative accounts for both pleasure and pain and says that they are both real, meaningful, and serve a greater overarching story with a good ending. In fact, there's more to life than simply seeking pleasures. The metanarrative explains pleasure and pain, but it doesn't tell a story that's *only about* pleasure and pain. There's more to it than these things. There's more to the meaning of life than these things.

PLEASURE AND THE PURPOSE OF HUMAN LIFE

Even if we are designed to experience pleasure in life (and that gives meaning to our pleasurable experiences), let's not confuse that with the *purpose* of life being for pleasure. We were designed to experience pleasure, but that's not the only thing we were designed to do, and the reality is that our ability to experience pleasure *is auxiliary* to our ultimate purpose. In other words, unlike the New Rich, our metanarrative can show that if we are not experiencing pleasures in life, that doesn't mean we're failing in life.

A helpful analogy might be God's design for marriage. God created marriage with an *essence,* and flowing from that essence come *blessings.* (The word *essence* means what's at the core of a thing's identity. If you take away a part of a thing's essence, it's no longer that thing.) Potential blessings that God intended for marriage include children, sexual pleasures, and companionship, to name a few. But if one of these blessings *doesn't* flow from a particular marriage, has that couple failed at marriage? Newlyweds or the infertile have no children but still have marriage. Illness, injury, or old age may limit a couple's sexual pleasures but they're still married.

Can you still have a marriage without robust companionship? Over their first 30 years of marriage, my dear friends Gerry and Doreen had grown to be each other's closest companions and confidants. But then in her 50s, Doreen had a major stroke, and as happens with some people, her personality drastically changed. She simply was no longer the companion she used to be. Irritable, often angry, sometimes verbally violent and combative, the stroke had traded in Gerry's close confidant for someone he at times couldn't even recognize. This can torture a spouse. In such painful circumstances, we might ask, "What's really left of that marriage?" But there is certainly something left. In fact, *everything* was left. Don't confuse the blessings with the essence.

The essence of marriage is *commitment*. God created marriage so that spouses would help and take care of each other. In so doing, they act as a dim mirror of how God takes care of us. (This is explicitly stated in the New Testament as the purpose of marriage for the Christian, in Ephesians 5:22-33.) Now, after Doreen's stroke, Gerry was called on more than ever to be a husband to his wife. And he did it brilliantly. He took care of her every need, watched over her at home until she needed to be moved to a facility, and then visited her several times a day, eventually moving into that same facility. The marriage was painful at times, but it was *meaningful*. Gerry had an opportunity, and he often took it, to be that dim mirror of Jesus' faithful love every day.

Apply this analogy to the ultimate purpose of human life in general. We've recognized that there are potential blessings that flow from being human in this world that God made (and that he still fills with his glory)—the potential blessing under discussion being *pleasure,* whether the pleasure derived from companionship, sunsets, adventure, or the like. But life's *potential blessings,* though part of God's design or intent (like the pleasures of sex he intended for marriage), are not life's *purpose.* The ultimate purpose of human life is not experiencing pleasure (or avoiding pain). God sums up the ultimate purpose of human life beautifully and clearly in his two Great Commandments: love God above all and love your neighbor as yourself. Notice: Just as the essence of marriage is *other*-focused, the purpose of human life is *other*-focused. Humans were created to love, to serve, to care, to be of benefit, and finally—just as God does—to find delight in bringing good into others' lives.

And so we're called to a life that ends up finding pleasure without living *for* it. This life of love brings us pleasure from three sources: knowing the biblical metanarrative, serving others, and pausing to simply enjoy the pleasures of life in God's world.

Regarding the first source: Once immersed in the biblical metanarrative, our greatest pleasure comes from being in a relationship with God, a fellowship (or communion) with him. Jesus spoke of the joy that comes from knowing him and from gathering with others who know him—joy that no one could take away (John 16:22). The apostle John, Jesus' dearest friend, once wrote (in a letter that became one of the books of the New Testament) about joy being made *complete* when a person not only learns about what Jesus has done for them but then shares this good news with others. John said his own joy was made complete by helping others find community with Jesus:

> **We proclaim to you what we have seen and heard, so that you also may have fellowship with us. And our fellowship is with the Father and with his Son, Jesus Christ. We write this to make our joy complete. (1 John 1:3,4)**

And so, in a very real sense, the greatest pleasures in life ("inexpressible and glorious" pleasures, 1 Peter 1:8) are found *in discovering the biblical metanarrative*—that there *is* a God who created us, loves us, and saved us; that there *is* hope for the future and a good, loving God in control—and in helping others recognize his love.

Regarding the second source: As John wrote, we also find service to other people pleasurable. That's what completes our joy: giving God's love a face and hands, sharing both his news and our lives with others. We begin seeing every other human being as we see ourselves within the biblical metanarrative: as created beings whom God values, loves, and entered into our world to save. We begin to find a unique sense of *pleasure in loving our neighbors as ourselves*, that is, in helping one another out and enjoying the new friendships and communities that follow. In fact, the very first Christians who gathered together are described as enjoying life like this:

> **All the believers were together and had everything in common. They sold property and possessions to give to anyone who had need. Every day they continued to meet together in the temple courts. They broke bread in their homes and ate together with glad and sincere hearts, praising God and enjoying the favor of all the people. (Acts 2:44-47)**

Note what kind of hearts they had. Not just generous. Not just sincere. But also glad. In one another's homes and cooking and company, they found pleasure.

Regarding the third source (the one on which Solomon focuses most in Ecclesiastes): We're called to take time and revel in the everyday pleasures of life as God in his providence allows us to experience them. Especially given the hardships we experience in life, God invites us to pause when the pleasures *do* come and to revel in them. Solomon himself says, "However many years anyone may live, let them enjoy them all. But let them remember the days of darkness, for there will be many" (Ecclesiastes 11:8). And, "I commend the enjoyment of life, because there is nothing better for a person under the sun than to eat and drink and be glad. Then joy will accompany them in their toil all the days of the life God has given them under the sun" (Ecclesiastes 8:15). We don't seek ultimate, transcendent, cosmic meaning in our pleasures, since the pleasures considered by themselves to be "under the sun" (apart from the biblical metanarrative), Solomon tells us, are meaningless.

But we can experience moments of pleasure as the brief moments they are—brief reminders that, given the cosmic meaning the biblical metanarrative gives us, life *is* beautiful. God *did* build us for pleasure. And so much more.

———————●———————

FOUR

WORK IS
MEANINGLESS

———— • ————

WALTER WHITE AND OZYMANDIAS

Andre was flipping out. "You're the one writing a book about meaninglessness, so you probably know what I feel like."

"No, Andre, researching and writing about a feeling isn't the same as having one. You gotta explain it to me."

We were sitting in his apartment. Andre had just gotten me a glass of water, and he was just beginning to peel the layers off and tell me what was really going on. Andre had accomplished several years of intense university performance, including several years earning a post-graduate degree, and all that was left was the thesis. But as he was working on his thesis, he became afflicted with extreme anxiety. All of a sudden, this high-output, focused, brilliant student wasn't allowed to do what made him most happy: work on his research. Somehow the pressures to perform flipped a switch, and he was forced to take several months off of finishing his thesis and several months off from anything that might cause stress. He found himself sitting at home, contributing nothing to his research. The longer he stayed away from his research, the more he began to feel purposeless and directionless. And the longer he felt purposeless and directionless, the more he began to show symptoms of clinical depression.

The only encouragement he had was the hope that, through enough tests, he'd be able to get his anxiety under control and be able to do his *work*. Without his work, "I feel empty most days . . . adrift." In other words, he felt like life was meaningless. He constantly expressed that he *knew* his life wasn't meaningless, but he couldn't help feeling that way. The importance of being productive, of having work to do, of having a project, can't be overlooked. In Western culture, I don't think it's an understatement to say that we largely view our value as humans and our meaningfulness in life in proportion to how important our work is. But this is a dangerous way to view ourselves. And every now and then, a philosopher or artist or writer tries to point this out.

An example: One of the most highly acclaimed television series of all time, *Breaking Bad*, revolves around the character of Walter White, a middle-class chemistry professor who, once he discovers he's dying of cancer, seeks to guarantee financial security for his family by producing and selling drugs. Soon, though, his motivation to deal drugs to secure his family's financial future morphs into a selfish desire to build some type of empire and legacy for himself. It's the ultimate midlife crisis gone horribly wrong.

Interestingly, the producers of the show created a trailer for the final season of *Breaking Bad* in which Bryan Cranston, the actor who plays Walter White, recites Percy Bysshe Shelley's "Ozymandias." Here's the poem:

> I met a traveller from an antique land
> Who said: "Two vast and trunkless legs of stone
> Stand in the desert. . . . Near them, on the sand,
> Half sunk, a shattered visage lies, whose frown,
> And wrinkled lip, and sneer of cold command,

Tell that its sculptor well those passions read
Which yet survive, stamped on these lifeless things,
The hand that mocked them and the heart that fed:
And on the pedestal these words appear:
'My name is Ozymandias, king of kings:
Look on my works, ye Mighty, and despair!'
Nothing beside remains. Round the decay
Of that colossal wreck, boundless and bare
The lone and level sands stretch far away."

The point of comparison for the television series is clear: The viewers of the final season will watch all that Walter White has built up for himself, all his work that he takes so much pride in, slowly fall apart around him. He will be humbled, and there will be nothing left of any value by which to remember Walter White.

Shelley's poem applies to far more than people dealing with midlife crises. He invites us to put the greatest figures of our own time in the place of Ozymandias (Ramesses II). We're to imagine statues of Bill Gates and Steve Jobs, presidents and prime ministers, Oprah and Beyoncé. Now picture a traveler thousands of years from now traversing a desert, stopping to read plaques proclaiming the vastness of the accomplishments of these people, only to look up at the stumpy remains of these monuments left amputated and misshapen by erosion. Shelley's point is clear: Given enough time, the accomplishments of *all* great people will eventually disappear.

There are two major issues with the future: The first is uncertainty. You have no idea what *everyone will do* with your legacy. The second is inevitability. One thing you do know for certain is that eventually *everyone will forget* about your legacy. Then one question remains: Was it worth it?

Shelley also invites us to consider our *own* desires to leave a legacy. If the great Ozymandias has left nothing behind but scraps, if there remains no memory of *his* great deeds, what chances are there that *our own* legacies will last?

Likewise, Solomon addresses our attempts to attain personal value through work, not just with the goal of the accumulation of wealth but also the desire to find meaning in life through "making a difference." Except Solomon will not have us compare ourselves to a Walter White or Ozymandias but to his own kingdom-building.

I MUST LEAVE THEM TO THE ONE WHO COMES AFTER ME

So I hated life, because the work that is done under the sun was grievous to me. All of it is meaningless, a chasing after the wind. I hated all the things I had toiled for under the sun, because I must leave them to the one who comes after me. And who knows whether that person will be wise or foolish? Yet they will have control over all the fruit of my toil into which I have poured my effort and skill under the sun. This too is meaningless. So my heart began to despair over all my toilsome labor under the sun. For a person may labor with wisdom, knowledge and skill, and then they must leave all they own to another who has not toiled for it. This too is meaningless and a great misfortune. What do people get for all the toil and anxious striving with which they labor under the sun? All their days their work is grief and pain; even at night their minds do not rest. This too is meaningless. (Ecclesiastes 2:17-23)

Ecclesiastes invites us again to imagine the vast wealth and accomplishments of the biblical Solomon. Like Shelley's poem, these observations hold true regardless of whether you have the traditional Solomon in mind. When we consider how Solomon is described in the Bible, we have the closest thing we can come to a biblical Ozymandias. We mentioned much earlier that Solomon accomplished some of the greatest kingdom-building feats in history. He built the First Temple of Israel, which was the Jewish version of Mecca's Al-Haram Mosque or the Vatican's St. Peter's Basilica. And if you compare the materials used in the temple with his own palace, as recorded in the Bible, his palace was of equal magnificence. And not only was Solomon a builder, but he also gained world renown as a scientist, a judge, and a ruler. He must have regularly burned the midnight oil, working hard to master his many vocations. As Solomon himself describes, "All their days their work is grief and pain; even at night their minds do not rest."

And when it came to building up all this knowledge, money, property, and legacy, he writes, "I hated all the things I had toiled for under the sun." Why? His first major reason for finding this toiling meaningless: "Because I must leave them to the one who comes after me." Let's remind ourselves that Solomon is speaking of life "under the sun," that is, forgetting that there's anything higher or beyond the simple daily experiences and drudgery of life in this sinful world. And if we measure ourselves entirely by what we accomplish in this life, the first major problem is *we don't get to keep it*. All our accomplishments remain ours for only a short time before they pass into the hands of someone else. As Solomon writes later in Ecclesiastes, "I have seen another evil under the sun, and it weighs heavily on mankind: God gives some people wealth, possessions and honor, so that they lack nothing their hearts desire, but God does not grant them the ability to enjoy them, and strangers enjoy them instead. This is meaningless, a grievous evil" (Ecclesiastes 6:1,2).

Remember a time when you took extra care to prepare your favorite meal or drink? A friend of mine, obsessed with coffee, will spend 30 minutes preparing the *perfect* cup of coffee, taking the time to grind the beans (that he may have just bought fresh an hour earlier at the corner roaster), to select a special brewing method, and then to hover over the pot so that the moment the coffee is done he can take it off the stove. After several steps, with each step anticipating more and more the cup of coffee and with the smell of brewing coffee intoxicating his nostrils, he finally lifts that *perfect* cup of coffee to his lips and then . . . a slip! It falls from his hands, and it spills. What is he thinking? What has just happened to that morning spent preparing his cup of coffee? Wasted, utterly wasted—the whole process seemingly meaningless. It would have been better if he had not even started brewing the cup of coffee. Now imagine that cup of coffee is your life's accomplishments, everything you worked for and stored up. But instead of dropping the cup, you die.

The difference, of course, is that the spilt coffee goes to no one, but all the fruit of your labor will go to others. Maybe the better analogy is that my friend spends his life preparing that perfect cup of coffee only to have *someone else* drink it, someone who can't tell good coffee from a cup of motor oil!

And, of course, many of us live knowing we'll never get to "drink the coffee." We spend considerable time working for our progeny, whether we're trying to create a better world for our immediate family only (like Walter White) or a better world for everyone (like Bill and Melinda Gates through their foundations). And you may have good reason to believe that what you leave behind will be used as you intended it for at least for a little while. But the problem remains, whether the legacy is for your children, community, or country: Even if, hypothetically, it was guaranteed that several generations would make good use of your legacy, it's all going to fade into nothing at some point and then be nothing for the eternity that follows. Everything eventually goes the way of Ozymandias' statue or, according to the Bible's favorite parallel picture, the flower of the field—beautiful one day but blown away the next, along with its memory.

UNCERTAINTY AND INEVITABILITY NOW

Solomon does offer a pragmatic response to the uncertainty of what will happen to your life's work after you die and the inevitability that it will one day be forgotten. His pragmatic response: Get short-term pleasure out of it. "A person can do nothing better than to eat and drink and find satisfaction in their own toil" (Ecclesiastes 2:24). In other words, find satisfaction *now* in what you do instead of focusing so much on the future. Again, Ecclesiastes isn't a treatise on how life can't be enjoyed. Of course it can be enjoyed, and it *should* be enjoyed! But recognize it for what it is. It's short-term.

And there are plenty of challenges in deriving short-term meaning out of your labor. Maybe you happen to have a decent job that you enjoy, a job that pays well, a job that makes you feel useful. Many people don't. What about them? Or again, Shelley and Solomon remind us that after we're gone, there's considerable uncertainty about how our legacy will be used, but it is inevitable that it will be forgotten. And we don't have to wait until after we die to experience the effects of this uncertainty and inevitability. We're not only uncertain about what happens after death; we're uncertain about what will happen tomorrow! It's not only inevitable that our work eventually will be forgotten after we die. It's inevitable that *during our present life* things we do will be forgotten.

If you've driven around Milwaukee, Wisconsin, in the past five years, you've maybe noticed once or twice a sticker, stuck to a light post here or a mailbox there, with a simple face and the phrase, "Have goals." Apparently, thousands of copies of this sticker grace the streets of Milwaukee, placed there by a Milwaukee street artist. What would motivate this kind of project, and why would it find such positive feedback from so many Milwaukee residents? In an interview, the artist said individuals have told him that his work has inspired them into "just grabbing the controls of their own life and making it be the thing that they want it to be. And then coming to me—finding me and telling me, 'It's because I saw this thing you put up.'"

The reason why even small phrases like "have goals" can be so powerful is clear: It is because they *do* generate meaning in a person's life. By simply having a goal, the actions in your life can be interpreted relative to how well they steer you toward or away from that goal. Goals mean meaning. At least short-term meaning. And so we're often trying to give our lives meaning by sketching out for ourselves goals, dreams, and future plans. After all, if we're working toward a goal, we have purpose: That future raise, getting a business started, saving up for that boat or summer cottage, getting that diploma. . . . You name the goal. And, of course, having dreams and aspirations is healthy! In clinical counseling, if someone is feeling depressed (and the feelings of depression aren't the direct result of a medical condition creating chemical imbalances), the first thing the counselor may ask is, "What are your goals in life?" And if the person doesn't have any, the counselor works with the person in creating a few goals. Feelings of depression often come from feeling purposeless and adrift in life, and so creating goals gives someone an actual trajectory for their life, which in turn will lessen the moments of depression.

The problem, though, is that if this is the *only* thing that gives your life trajectory, if your own personal goals are the only things that you derive purpose from, you're still in for a largely depressing life. Because no one just hands out fulfilled dreams. No one will ask you what your goals are and drop you off there. Even hard work doesn't guarantee anything. Whether you'll get anywhere near those goals is uncertain from the start. As Solomon says, "Since no one knows the future, who can tell someone else what is to come?" (Ecclesiastes 8:7). Or even more to the point:

> I have seen something else under the sun:
> The race is not to the swift
>   or the battle to the strong,
> nor does food come to the wise
>   or wealth to the brilliant
>   or favor to the learned;
> but time and chance happen to them all. (Ecclesiastes 9:11)

You can't control the economy or world affairs, every aspect of your health, or the decisions of the people around you. You can't predict all the hardships or roadblocks or hurdles you or your children are going to face. Writer and journalist Ta-Nehisi Coates describes his grief and anger over the alleged murder of a college acquaintance of his at the hands of police. The murder victim, named Prince Jones, was a very well-liked, Christian young man who was from a well-to-do family and had a fiancée and a young daughter. Coates has a poignant description of what that murder cost Jones' family. It's an impressive portrait of how meaningless a Christian parent's efforts and expenses can end up being "under the sun" because of their child's sudden, unjust death:

> Think of all the love poured into him. Think of the tuitions for Montessori and music lessons. Think of the gasoline expended, the treads worn carting him to football games, basketball tournaments, and Little League. Think of the time spent regulating sleepovers. Think of the surprise birthday parties, the daycare, and the reference checks on babysitters. Think of *World Book* and *Childcraft*. Think of checks written for family photos. Think of credit cards charged for vacations. Think of soccer balls, science kits, chemistry sets, racetracks, and model trains. Think of all the embraces, all the private jokes, customs, greetings, names, dreams, all the shared knowledge and capacity of a black family injected into that vessel of flesh and bone. And think of how that vessel was taken, shattered on the concrete, and all its holy contents, all that had gone into him, sent flowing back to the earth.[34]

You can anticipate *some* stuff; you can be relatively in control of your life compared to the lives of others, but you *will not* reach all your dreams. Your children will not reach all your dreams for them, perhaps tragically they will not even reach any. And so, if you derive all your value and purpose in life in how well you (or your dear children) achieve goals, you're at best gambling and most realistically looking forward to bouts of depressive experiences.

And what happens when you're at a point in your life when you are past setting goals and dreams? Marion was 100 years old, of very poor health (as well as nearly blind and deaf). She was often cranky with me. She didn't want to live anymore. She told me this one way or another every time I visited her. "Why is the man upstairs keeping me around?" she would always say. And every time I answered her with a smile, "To teach me patience." Marion couldn't see a purpose for herself because she had run out of goals, dreams, and future plans. And it made sense. For most of us, if we don't have goals, dreams, and plans, we feel like we don't have a purpose, which means we don't have a *meaningful* existence. Marion simply went one step farther, as many Christians find themselves doing. She thought that the reason *God* keeps people around is to do things, and unless she was doing something for God, there wasn't any reason for her to be around. She slipped into thinking about God like many people do, seeing God as an exalted boss with goals and an agenda, a God who views people primarily as employees he's going to put to work to achieve those goals and fulfill that agenda.

Of course, God still *did* have a purpose for Marion, and that purpose did involve doing things, even if she couldn't see it. Because God didn't see Marion as his employee. The God of the Bible sees us differently. It's more relational, remember? Our purpose is to love: to love God and other people. And just like a spouse shouldn't see loving his wife as *work*, something he can clock in and out of, God calls us to see our purpose as something far more profound than work. And it's our goal to see ourselves that way too.

WHOEVER LOVES MONEY NEVER HAS ENOUGH MONEY

We will come back to the idea of "have goals." But often we find ourselves doing our jobs *not* because we're pursuing some meaningful (to us) life goals. Often we do our jobs simply because we want the *money*.

Most people recognize that acquiring money isn't acquiring happiness. Yet, on some level, we agree with comedian Groucho Marx: "While money can't buy happiness, it certainly lets you choose your own form of misery." In other words, we *know* money can't buy happiness, but often enough that's how we live! It's a subtle form of believing that money can give us things of value in this life. And, again, you certainly can argue that money affects your ability to acquire things with short-term meaning. The trouble is when we live as though money will give us cosmic meaning. Solomon writes:

> Whoever loves money never has enough;
>> whoever loves wealth is never satisfied with their income.
>> This too is meaningless.
> As goods increase, . . . what benefit are they to the owners
>> except to feast their eyes on them? (Ecclesiastes 5:10,11)

If you're acquiring money in order to be happy or to feel like you have some type of cosmic, transcendent value in this universe, you'll never get enough money. You'll keep telling yourself, "A little more . . . ," and then you'll get the meaningful life you want, but a little more is never enough to give it to you. Famously, John D. Rockefeller Sr. (who tops many lists of the wealthiest Americans of all time) on his deathbed was asked how much money was enough, and he responded, "A little bit more."

The reason, of course, is because money in and of itself is cosmically meaningless, as Solomon says. What gives us meaning beyond ourselves can only come from one thing: a story that comes from beyond us but that includes us. And if you want your life to be part of a *good* story, you can't buy that. You can only be invited into it, as the biblical God has invited you. Money, though, is of no benefit, except simply to fill your eyes on a feast that will never fill your belly.

Now that certainly doesn't mean money is of no use to us. Of course it is. It's great for financial security, helping others, and short-term enjoyment and pleasure. But don't expect it to be of any use in giving you a meaningful life. It's simply not that kind of thing. You'll have to lift your eyes higher.

THE MYTH OF SISYPHUS

The "have goals" crowd would agree with this: Don't just live for the next paycheck or the next Cyber Monday deals. Be intentional. Be purposeful. Make something of your life.

Can we?

A group of atheist thinkers in the 20th century who we now label the *French existentialists* (not to be confused with the people earlier labeled existentialists, Kierkegaard and Dostoevsky, who were Christians) asserted that we can and must do just this. Philosophers like Jean-Paul Sartre and Simone de Beauvoir asked, If there is no God, and so no one to create us with a meaningful essence, can we *create* for ourselves a meaningful essence through the choices we make? And isn't that our only option?

They all agreed that, if there is no God, humans are born into an absurd situation, one in which we *want* our lives to have cosmic meaning but instead everything begins meaningless. The French existentialists made a point of frankly and honestly admitting their belief in the non-existence of God, the resulting cosmic meaninglessness of life, and the struggle with absurdity that follows. Albert Camus (he didn't like being labeled an *existentialist,* but we still call him one today) wrote a novel titled *The Outsider* (in some translations *The Stranger*), which involved a protagonist, Mercault, who shot a man and was now on trial. At one point Mercault muses in his cell:

> I'd been right, I was still right, I was always right. I'd lived in a certain way and I could just as well have lived in a different way. I'd done this and I hadn't done that. I hadn't done one thing whereas I had done another. So what? It was as if I'd been waiting all along for this very moment and for the early dawn when I'd be justified. Nothing, nothing mattered and I knew very well why. . . . From the depths of my future, throughout the whole of this absurd life I'd been leading, I'd felt a vague breath drifting towards me across all the years

that were still to come, and on its way this breath had evened out everything that was then being proposed to me in the equally unreal years I was living through. What did other people's deaths or a mother's love matter to me, what did his God or the lives people chose or the destinies they selected matter to me?[35]

Mercault feels he is being honest that, if his worldview is correct that God is dead, this life is "*absurd.*" "Nothing, nothing mattered." In his afterword to the novel, Camus wrote that the real reason Mercault was on trial was "because he doesn't play the game . . . he refuses to lie."[36] The game, of course, is living as if the death of God doesn't matter, living like those whom Nietzsche's madman was trying to warn. But if we're completely honest about life, if there's only "under the sun," in the words of the Teacher, it's all meaningless.

The master metaphor for this absurd life became, for the French existentialists, the Greek myth of Sisyphus, a story in which the gods condemned a man to forever push a rock up a hill, but the rock would simply roll down to the bottom again the moment he arrived at the top. This is the life we are born into, they argued. Instead of finding ourselves in the midst of a story where there is a hopeful beginning and an end that we look forward to, we find ourselves in an uncaring universe and faced with purposeless, meaningless, and never-ending striving. Albert Camus, who first used Sisyphus as a metaphor, writes:

> The gods had condemned Sisyphus to ceaselessly rolling a rock to the top of a mountain, whence the stone would fall back of its own weight. They had thought with some reason that there is no more dreadful punishment than futile and hopeless labor. . . .
>
> You have already grasped that Sisyphus is the absurd hero. He *is,* as much through his passions as through his fortune. His scorn of the gods, his hatred of death, and his passion for life won him that unspeakable penalty in which the whole

> being is exerted toward accomplishing nothing. This is the price that must be paid for the passions of this earth. . . .
>
> Sisyphus teaches the higher fidelity that negates the gods and raises rocks. He too concludes that all is well. This universe henceforth without a master seems to him neither sterile nor futile. Each atom of that stone, each mineral flake of that night-filled mountain, in itself forms a world. The struggle itself toward the heights is enough to fill a man's heart. One must imagine Sisyphus happy.[37]

Despite Camus' honesty about life being meaningless and absurd without God, somehow his Sisyphus can conclude, in the midst of an absurd life, within a world "without a master" (that is, without God), that "all is well." How? The struggle. "The struggle itself toward the heights is enough to fill a man's heart." Somehow the struggle itself can give meaningful purpose to one's life. According to Camus, the fact that Sisyphus has a choice to push or not push that rock gives his life meaning. Perhaps your choices are not ultimately meaningful to the universe, but the matter stands that *you have a choice.* Your sentience and autonomy make you able to choose, and those choices are yours and yours alone, and these choices that are yours and yours alone change the world, even if only a small part of it for only a short period of time. According to Camus, the gods thought they were punishing Sisyphus, but the fact of the matter is that they were liberating him.

Do you buy it? Many people do, with or without the French philosophers. I may not be able to control *everything* but, as William Ernest Henley inspires in his well-known poem "Invictus," "It matters not how strait the gate, / How charged with punishments the scroll, / I am the master of my fate, / I am the captain of my soul." In other words, I can control *me, my* fate, *my* mark on this world. From Churchill to Mandela, we've rallied behind Henley's words, or morphs of it: Frank Sinatra's anthem croons, "I did it my way." And although the singer grew to hate the song, people love to croon along with it, from genocide-accused Serbian dictators to grieving funeral-planners.

Regardless of the ultimate implications of Camus' line of thinking or its morale-boosting appeal, we know (and Camus knew) that it can't give us what we're looking for: a *truly cosmic (transcendent) meaningful life.* If there is no God, there's simply no overarching story to be a part of and we certainly can't create an overarching story through our choices. We're left, again, with short-term meaning. What we do has a certain amount of value for us and for those around us, but every day, every hour, every minute that passes after a choice has been made, the effects of that choice are diminishing, again, like the face of Ozymandias. Whereas Sisyphus was condemned to an *eternity* of meaningless toil, if the atheist is correct, ours is only for a *short lifetime,* and then it's over, along with our ability to make choices and our ability to bring short-term meaning into this world.

IS PROGRESS POSSIBLE?

At this point, the skeptic might be saying, "Okay, I agree money can't buy happiness, and I agree that if there is no God, life is absurd. And so the choices I make in this world can't give me cosmic meaning. . . . But I can at least work toward making the world a better place, right? That's meaningful, isn't it?"

I remember a few years ago when I was starting to formulate some of these thoughts; I was trying to explain to an agnostic friend of mine the need for God in order for life to be meaningful. He and his partner were extremely politically active; they were both urban planners deeply interested in revitalizing segregated, economically depressed neighborhoods. At one point he quickly turned to me and said, "So if there's no God, there's no point in the work we do? There's no point in trying to make our cities better places to live? There's no point in trying to improve the lives of people in the world? You're saying our work is meaningless?"

I was caught off guard, wrapped up in my own lines of reasoning, and I hadn't realized how he was reading this all. I deeply offended him. To make things worse, I didn't have a good answer at the time. I don't know if our friendship ever quite recovered.

If I could rewind the clock, this is what I would have wanted to say: "Of course it's meaningful. Of course throwing yourself into work that you conscientiously believe is good for your community is awesome. Of course that's what life is all about. You *know* it's meaningful. The question, though, is *why* is it meaningful? Because there are people who don't care about their communities, who take no interest in their neighbors, who are comfortable with their selfish lifestyles. Would you tell them what they're doing is *wrong,* that they're not doing what they're supposed to be doing? And then what would you say determines that they are wrong?" I'd challenge him to see his meaningful work within a larger, meaningful story that would give it not only temporal, short-term meaning but cosmic, eternal, transcendent meaning.

Remember that the point of this book is not to prove to you that your life is meaningless. I certainly don't think it is. I think every life has infinite value, that every choice we make has deep significance, and that there's tremendous value, even *cosmic* value, in trying to make the world a better place through the work we do.

The question is not, "Is your life meaningful?" The question is, "Can you give an explanation for why your life is meaningful?"

And Solomon's response is, if we're only looking at life "under the sun"—that is, life as it daily appears to us in all its monotony, pain, suffering, and temporariness—if we're not seeing our life within a higher, overarching story, we have no good reason to believe life is meaningful. However, the overarching story, the *metanarrative* of the biblical God, infuses every bit of life with transcendent, lasting, infinite meaning. Does a part of you feel like you were created to love and care for fellow human beings? Looking at life "under the sun" will not give you an explanation for that feeling. But the biblical metanarrative does: A good God who loves us created us to do just that, to love, both him and one another. And the highest expression of his love for us is found in his giving his life for us on the cross, an act that both unites us with God and provides the proper motivation for us to give our lives for others. Does a part of you feel like you were created to make this world a better place, that if you're just wasting your life away in front of the TV or computer, you really are, somehow, *wasting* your life? Looking at life "under the sun" will not give you an explanation for that feeling. But the biblical metanarrative does: The Bible teaches that humans brought pain and suffering first into this world through wrong choices, but God through history has redeemed us and calls us now to work toward making this world a better place, first and foremost through sharing the good news of the gospel metanarrative.

Most everyone agrees we should be working for progress. The question, though, is can you explain both *why* we should be working for progress and *what* that progress should look like? Considering life only "under the sun" can't give us answers. As the Christian writer G. K. Chesterton wrote at the beginning of the 20th century, at a time where nationalistic progress (expanding one's nation in order to bring more order and "civility" into the world) was all the rage:

> **Progress by its very name indicates a direction; and the moment we are in the least doubtful about the direction, we become in the same degree doubtful about the progress. Never perhaps since the beginning of the world has there been an age that had less right to use the word "progress" than we.**[38]

During Chesterton's lifetime, the ability for one nation (like his own British nation) to affect the whole world through trade, warfare, and the spread of culture was growing at the exact same time as the secularization of academic thought (that is, leaving God out of philosophy, psychology, the sciences, and all academic subjects—exactly what Nietzsche was talking about when he spoke of the death of God). Academics and artists wanted to make the world a better place, wanted to aid the progress of civilization. The problem, though, as Chesterton points out, is that when we take God completely out of the conversation, if we're trying to explain everything only in naturalistic terms, we can't really talk about progress. How can we talk about moral progress if, given an evolutionary explanation for all things, there's no such thing as objective morality to measure that progress against? What, then, do we actually mean by the word *progress?* How can we talk about scientific progress if, given an evolutionary explanation for all things, there's no ultimate aim or transcendent purpose for the existence of humans? How can we talk about political progress if, given an evolutionary explanation for all things, we can't objectively make a value distinction between good and bad governments? (To use an extreme example, how can you *know* that Hitler was bad for humanity and it's not just your opinion? He certainly thought he was progressing the human race!)

Given an atheistic, evolutionary view of the world, you cannot talk objectively about progress. Things just are. Remember Hume's guillotine. If we get our knowledge only from what we can observe, we can only make fact statements, not "ought" statements. We can't just call something "progress" and say this is the direction in which we *should* be going.

But if we see life within the biblical metanarrative, we can talk in those "should" and "ought" ways. As Chesterton says elsewhere, "Without the doctrine of the Fall, all idea of progress is unmeaning." The Bible tells us that this is a story in which *things are not as they should be*. We have already discussed how Solomon himself writes, "God created mankind upright, but they have gone in search of many schemes" (Ecclesiastes 7:29). Because of the fall, that is, because of humanity's first rejection of God's love, so very many things now need to be set right in this world.

And because God has given us all consciences that tell us (albeit imperfectly) how things *should be,* even people who don't know the Story have the ability to make meaningful choices that God desires—choices that help to set things right. We have the ability to see this as a world in which progress is desperately needed, and our consciences tell us we ought to be engaged in that progress.

Solomon echoes the Bible's clearly stated diagnosis that it won't be possible to recreate the Garden of Eden, to make a world free of political corruption, famine and poverty, abuse and neglect, inequality, and pollution. He reminds us, "What is crooked cannot be straightened; what is lacking cannot be counted" (Ecclesiastes 1:15). We won't be able to comfort every victim: "I saw the tears of the oppressed—and they have no comforter; power was on the side of their oppressors—and they have no comforter" (4:1). We won't get rid of injustice entirely: "If you see the poor oppressed in a district, and justice and rights denied, do not be surprised at such things" (5:8). We won't make a perfect government: "There is an evil I have seen under the sun, the sort of error that arises from a ruler: Fools are put in many high positions" (10:5,6). Still, Solomon says, we ought to know that these situations are in fact "evil." They are worth deploring. Therefore, we could rightly conclude that we indeed ought to be seeking out better ways to govern, better ways to deal with famine and poverty, better ways to deal with emotionally and psychologically broken people, better ways to encourage the respect of women in the workplace, better ways to take care of the environment—you name it. This helps our neighbors. This undoes evil. This is progress.

But Solomon does not draw that conclusion in Ecclesiastes. He does not issue such a call for progress. The Teacher pulls no punches in his assessment of the problems of this world, problems that cripple even the very institutions that should be working justice: "In the place of judgment—wickedness was there" (3:16). Yet instead of responding with an ethic of working against oppression, injustice, and violence (which Solomon could have provided; his book of

Proverbs has a good deal of this kind of encouragement), his goal here is to lift our gaze higher, above the things "under the sun," to think more deeply than simply about *how to fix things.* God's understanding of progress is far greater and far more epic than we could ever imagine.

The all-too-evident pain and suffering we see in this world (a topic we explored at length in the previous chapter)—the evil that humans commit against one another and the general hardships of life—are signs that there's actually a deeper problem. The reason things are not as they should be between us fellow humans is because things are not as they should be between us and God: that fall did not simply bring pain and suffering into the midsts of our relationships with one another, but it brought a divide into our relationship with God. Our whole race walked away from God's love. Real progress, then, begins with *that* relationship being restored—finding that love again in the face of Jesus. Restored to God's love, understanding the Story of his love for our world, we see everything and everyone with new eyes. In the midst of all this world's pain and suffering, we see glimpses of the richness and beauty God wanted humanity to enjoy all along. *But also* we begin to understand so much more deeply why we desire to bring even more richness and beauty into our pained and suffering neighbors' lives. We begin to understand how God has placed us as agents within this world to reflect his love for us through how we love one another. The healing this can bring to our lives (or to our world) is far from perfect. We still carry within us the selfish natures of our parents who first rebelled against God. And that part of us still—just like our first parents—would always rather play God than enjoy (and spread) God's love. But God presses on. He does not stop working to motivate us to be his healers. He does not stop appreciating even our smallest acts of healing. He does not stop delighting whenever another hurting human is brought to recognize his love—this delight is, after all, what he created the world for. And he himself, even through the pain and suffering of this world, does not stop working toward a good ending for our Story.

WORK IS MEANINGFUL

Back to 100-year-old Marion. She didn't know why God was keeping her alive. But because she was a Christian, deep down she knew she didn't need to know the reason herself. Instead, because she knew there *is* a God who is working through history for all his beloved children, including her, I encouraged her that she certainly had meaningful work to do. But the key is that meaning in life for the Christian doesn't flow from doing work. Rather, think of it the other way around: We know all the work we do is meaningful because it flows out of God's metanarrative. God makes the whole universe meaningful, and so the work within it *has to be* meaningful. We are not meaningful *because* we work. We work because we are meaningful, living within a meaningful world. Or another way: it isn't our work that gives our story meaning. It's our story that gives our work meaning.

The Bible teaches Christians that all the work they do in life is of the greatest importance. There's no such thing as work that is insignificant, random, or of small consequence. But what is the nature of this significance? Is it something that the work of non-Christians has too and they're just unaware of it? Or does becoming a Christian add new meaning to one's work that wasn't there before? It is both. God's hand is working through people in two ways.

The first is what's called God's *providence:* God has oversight over all things, moving them toward his good ending, and this involves working through the choices people make to take care of people. The food we eat is given to us by God, but through farmers, grocery cashiers, and those who prepare our food. And so when the farmer, cashier, and cook do their work—whether they care about God or not—they're taking part in God's overarching care of the people of this world. He's literally at work through them. Their work, therefore, is part of a *cosmic* story and thus has cosmic meaning. The same goes for the doctors who seek our good health, the government workers who give us security, and the teachers who give us an education. *All* the people in your life who give you these things are taking part in God's plan of caring for you and meeting your needs. *Provid-ence* is about *provid-ing*. It's God's way of working through all of us to give us *good* things (James 1:17).

When people do things clearly *wrong*—when the doctor slacks and gives bad advice, when the government worker uses power for evil ends, and when the teacher neglects students—even though God is not the author of that evil (evil is an *action* that these individuals chose to carry out; it is not something *created* by God), God in his providence, as the Bible teaches, works through these events, like the evil in the plotline of a story, toward his good ending. He promises an ending where both justice wins and God's love reigns. And so this means God is working even through *your* terrible choices. Remember, this is a meta*narrative* we're talking about—a story, *the* Story. And though there's evil that must be dealt with within the story, God makes sure it *all* serves his narrative's purpose. I once heard a professional psychologist and Christian put it this way to a young woman struggling with her traumatic past: "God does not waste darkness." Even the dark moments of our life—although he never wanted them—God will use to bring an unimaginable amount of light into this world. He will use them to make "everything beautiful in its time" (Ecclesiastes 3:11).

And when the farmer, cashier, or cook discovers this Story, God's rescue plan, she discovers something else: God has been using *her* all along too. God has been using her through his providence to give *good* things. Her work is important. Her work is part of the God of the universe's plan. Her work has *meaning*. And the meaning was there in the work all along because God was using it all along. But how much more satisfying the work is when you *know* God is using it for good!

That's God's providence. But there's another way Christians can see everything they do in life as significant. Providence is about God's guidance over all of human history. What we're going to talk about next is how God especially uses Christians to carry out some of that providential work—work done now in his name, for his name, by his agents.

The Bible teaches that Jesus died for all people, to bring all imperfect humans back into union with a perfect God. And so the story of our lives and of all history is God working out this rescue mission, this undoing of the enemy's discord. And so when a person finds out how God has rescued them and brought them back into union with him, their life is no longer the same. With this new knowledge, the person is someone new, and that new identity changes the way she sees what she does in the world. She sees herself functioning, as the Bible calls it, as "God's handiwork, created in Christ Jesus to do good works, which God prepared in advance for us to do" (Ephesians 2:10). In other words, Christians function as *rescued* and *reclaimed* and *redesigned* children of God—children who have learned through the Bible who their Father is, how they've been brought back into his family, and how he has now given them work to do on his behalf *as* his family. What we now *are* in Christ (a new creation) radically changes how we understand what we *do* for God (good works prepared in *advance*). And if this work has been prepared in *advance,* we know it is not random, inconsequential, or without purpose. The Master Storyteller has written the good works into the story for a *purpose*. And that purpose is incomprehensibly meaningful.

This work has been called being a *mask of God,* that is, God making himself known to the world through Christians living out their lives. Or call it being the *hands and feet* of Jesus. Christians, now knowing the great acts of love Jesus has shown them through his rescue mission of self-sacrifice, want to mirror that love through their lives.

That work is broad, from doing as best as you can the work within all your roles in life (sister, brother, father, mother, employee, employer, neighbor, citizen, etc.) to especially sharing the good news of God's metanarrative of salvation, that God sent Jesus to save us. The former work Christians call their *vocation,* that is, the specific work God has called us to do in this world. (We'll talk a bit more about this in the next chapter.) And maybe this work looks the same as what they were doing before they became Christians. But God says it's not: It's new work prepared for the Christian to do *as a Christian,* that is, as a mask of Christ. The latter work the Bible calls sharing the *gospel,* a fancy way of saying you are simply telling people what God has done for us through Jesus.

And so Christians believe every sleeping and waking moment is a gift from God to be his mask, his hands and feet. We believe God is working through all people for our good (despite the evil and suffering we've created), but we also believe God has called each Christian to do special work as his agent of love in this world.

That is how Christians understand their work within God's gospel metanarrative. Without the biblical God, as Solomon says, it's all ultimately meaningless: there's no possible good ending to contextualize the work we do, and there's no overarching good story that gives our work transcendent meaning. Given atheism, we just *are,* and so our work is valueless with no trajectory, like endlessly rolling a stone up a hill. Given a typical religion where the goal is to appease an angry god, our work is insufficient, hopelessly imperfect, and so has no hopeful future. But the Bible teaches the opposite. Our work can feel meaningful because God has built us to do meaningful work for him—work that we're not required to do to get on his team, but work *gifted* to us to do because he's already done everything to get us on his team. Through Christ it's possible to rediscover the work we do out of love for a Saving God and therefore find that work transcendently, cosmically meaningful.

Return to that young woman and the Christian psychologist. "God does not waste darkness." The psychologist actually meant it to hit the woman in two ways: On the one hand, her past traumatic pain is not meaningless and accidental. God will use it. On the other hand, how is he going to use it? After weeks of counseling and healing, the young woman and I talked often about what that psychologist said. The young woman said to me, "I know I can now help others find meaning in their similar trauma." And as her pastor and friend, I had the honor of watching her do just that with many people for many years. God uses it *all* through his providence for *good*. And that means God uses *you* for good.

C. S. Lewis wrote, "He who has God and everything else has no more than he who has God only."[39] Lewis' bold claim is that everything we try to accumulate in this world has no value at all, at least in comparison to having God. Solomon learned this the hard way. Hopefully it won't need to be as hard for us to learn.

————— • —————

CHAPTER

HUMAN LIFE IS
MEANINGLESS

————— • —————

THE QUESTION

It was a drawing of a man shooting himself in the head.

I wasn't prepared for the amount of pain, suffering, and despair I was going to help people through as a pastor. I had great seminary training; they worked hard to get us ready. And for a while I felt ready. The first couple marriages falling apart, the first handful of times sitting at bedsides and watching people die, the first dozen or so addictions, . . . but at some point *their* trauma becomes *your* trauma.

And this one was traumatizing, not because of how unique it was but because of the realization of how *un-unique* it was, how endemic, how overwhelming the pain and suffering that people go through in our culture was becoming for me.

He was smart, polite, a hard worker, an "ideas" man. But he had no current job, no friends, no girlfriend, no reason to get up in the morning. In an e-mail, he shared with me a scanned page from his journal with that drawing subtitled, "No purpose = no reason to go on."

I knew he wasn't the only person in my church family who felt this way at times. We live in a time of tremendous loneliness. Surveys regularly find that in North America a high percentage of people have no close friends or confidants. The amount of people living alone is rising dramatically. (US stats: 5 percent of the population in the 1920s, up to 27 percent as of 2013.)[40] Among other factors, social media technology is having the opposite effect from what we had anticipated: because of the growing lack of face-to-face social encounters, people are feeling *more* isolated. This culture obviously is creating a host of problems and negative effects, one of which we're particularly interested in: Less social interaction means less apparent meaning in one's life. Remember short-term meaning? It is derived from someone *valuing* something or someone else. And so the less people value *you,* the effect is feeling that you are *less valuable.*

That e-mail was the beginning of a long process. We would have to address the short-term meaning: time to get a job, friends, a reason to get up in the morning. But at some point we would have to address the picture he had drawn. If the caption he put under it was correct, then the deeper questions were: Do you not have a purpose? Is a person's purpose in life contingent entirely on whether or not you *feel* like you have a purpose or on whether you're valued by other people?

But the drawing. I can't get it out of my head.

A recent Brigham Young University meta-analysis of research done on social isolation found that loneliness increases your risk of death by 30 percent. Some studies say 60 percent. This is for biological and practical reasons but also psychological ones. "It's safe to say that while not all lonely people are suicidal, all suicidal people are lonely."[41]

And yet it isn't only the socially isolated who muse about dying. At the heart of what it means to be human is the contemplation of death. And, to some extent, it comes naturally to us. The oldest records of humanity involve the contemplation of death, and our greatest works of art explore this human condition—exploring our ability to think about our own mortality in deep and profound ways and exploring the logical options that death poses for humans.

> To be, or not to be—that is the question:
> Whether 'tis nobler in the mind to suffer
> The slings and arrows of outrageous fortune
> Or to take arms against a sea of troubles
> And by opposing end them. To die, to sleep—
> No more—and by a sleep to say we end
> The heartache, and the thousand natural shocks
> That flesh is heir to. 'Tis a consummation
> Devoutly to be wished. To die, to sleep—
> To sleep—perchance to dream: ay, there's the rub,
> For in that sleep of death what dreams may come
> When we have shuffled off this mortal coil,
> Must give us pause. There's the respect
> That makes calamity of so long life.

In the West, one of our most memorable examples of this is Hamlet's soliloquy on death (from the pen of William Shakespeare). Prince Hamlet knows he's being watched. And so he's keeping up a ruse he's been working on for some time, pretending he's out of his mind and on the brink of killing himself. He's already convinced his mom, and now he's trying to convince his enemies. He speaks these words as his enemies listen. And so, in Hamlet's mind, these are the questions he thinks a suicidal person would wrestle with. He begins with the now-famous words: "To be, or not to be." Hamlet is asking, "Should I live, or not?" Should he continue his struggle in life, or is it okay to die? Is life worth suffering "the slings and arrows of outrageous fortune," that is, is it worth suffering through the pain and torment of a life often filled with seemingly random justice and injustice? Or should he die? In death, the slings and arrows, the "sea of troubles," and the "thousand natural shocks" all humans experience come to an end.

Or do they? "There's the rub." Because what waits for us after death? Is it simply an endless sleep, the end of all consciousness, self-awareness, and existence? Or is there more? "What dreams may come"? If death's sleep is not the end to our experiences, does it bring good or bad "dreams"? If bad "dreams" await (at least, dreams worse than our experiences in this life), it's worth struggling with every fiber to stay alive as long as possible. If good dreams await, then the journey does not have to be feared. How do we answer this question? It "must give us pause." In other words, Hamlet suggests that how we answer this question matters. Not only does the answer inform us for how we are to live *now* (either in eager expectation or in dread for that coming moment), but it also has deep implications on the meaning of life and the value of human life.

If there's even a slim chance that how we live in this life affects the next, this ought to "give us pause." If there's no chance that anything waits for us, so that our consciousness and all we have experienced is simply extinguished forever like any other conscious organism in this universe, then this too ought to "give us pause."

Thousands of years before Hamlet, Solomon wrote his own poetry on how to understand the "slings and arrows of outrageous fortune." And at the heart of it, Solomon, like Shakespeare, brings in death. If, like the atheist suggests, both humans and animals go to the same place after death, Solomon declares that human life is meaningless. Is he right?

THE DEAD ARE HAPPIER THAN THE LIVING

I saw something else under the sun:
In the place of judgment—wickedness was there,

> **in the place of justice—wickedness was there.**
> **(Ecclesiastes 3:16)**

Psychologists are now warning parents not to allow their young children to watch the news. Studies seem to be demonstrating that the violence children see on the news has more lasting effects than the violence seen in fictional shows and movies. I remember when my own five-year-old son became obsessed with "bad" people in the world, especially possible criminals in our neighborhood. The sense of injustice in the world is overwhelming—the fact that crime pays, that "in the place of justice—wickedness [is] there." Solomon is telling us nothing novel here—bad things happen to people trying to do good and good things happen to people trying to do evil, people become rich and powerful off the exploitation of others, and so often honesty doesn't seem to get us far in life. And this injustice has lasting effects on how we develop as humans and on how we experience the world. This is a major theme in Ecclesiastes.

And it's a theme made even more poignant because it claims to have been written by a man renowned for dispensing justice in his court. Recall Solomon's reputation and how the Teacher has him speak: One of antiquity's most legendary magnates calls riches meaningless. One of antiquity's most legendary intellectuals calls wisdom meaningless. Now one of antiquity's most legendary judges calls the world ultimately unjust.

In ancient Israel, the king was also the nation's supreme court and chief justice. Solomon's verdicts, sifting through even the most baffling criminal trials, are said to have put the whole country "in awe, because they saw that he had wisdom from God to administer justice" (1 Kings 3:28). And now this judge says wickedness reigns. He even goes so far as to say that the world is so wicked and unjust, you're better off *dead*.

> **Again I looked and saw all the oppression**
> **that was taking place under the sun:**

> I saw the tears of the oppressed—
>   and they have no comforter;
> power was on the side of their oppressors—
>   and they have no comforter.
> And I declared that the dead,
>   who had already died,
> are happier than the living,
>   who are still alive.
> But better than both
>   is the one who has never been born,
> who has not seen the evil
>   that is done under the sun. (Ecclesiastes 4:1-3)

Again, visceral words from Solomon: The dead are better off than the living. Why? Because the dead no longer experience the injustice of this world. And Solomon goes even one step further: Better than both the dead and the living is "the one who has never been born," that is, the person who hasn't yet even been alive. Why? Because the living are experiencing injustice, and the dead have already experienced a life full of injustice. It is only the unborn who have been truly free from injustice, who have not "seen the evil that is done under the sun," who have not been jaded by life like our children watching the news, seeing bullies get away without discipline, and feeling the unprovoked or unjustified wrath of a parent.

Too much oppression. Too many tears. Yet Solomon admits that he personally believes a time is coming when things will be set right, when justice will have its way:

> I said to myself,
> "God will bring into judgment
>   both the righteous and the wicked,
> for there will be a time for every activity,
>   a time to judge every deed." (Ecclesiastes 3:17)

There is a judgment day in the Teacher's metanarrative. But it is as if he would not be in a hurry to find any comfort in that knowledge.

It is as if he says, *I understand that this doesn't do you a lot of good right now. That this doesn't make life any better. Someday-justice doesn't make this present world any less cruel or less bitter.* Because in almost the very next sentence, Solomon writes this:

DUST, ANIMALS, INDIFFERENCE

Surely the fate of human beings is like that of the animals; the same fate awaits them both: As one dies, so dies the other. All have the same breath; humans have no advantage over animals. Everything is meaningless. All go to the same place; all come from dust, and to dust all return. Who knows if the human spirit rises upward and if the spirit of the animal goes down into the earth?

So I saw that there is nothing better for a person than to enjoy their work, because that is their lot. For who can bring them to see what will happen after them? (Ecclesiastes 3:19-22)

We can see clearly that we are like the animals. How? "The same fate awaits them both." In other words, the experiences of humans are not all that different from the experiences of animals in that we both live, then die, and then "all go to the same place; all come from dust, and to dust all return." Sometimes a pet and its owner even share the same coffin.

And remember that Solomon brings this all up as part of his discussion on how our lives reek with injustice. It is as if Solomon would say, *Observation of the animal world goes a long way to show us that transcendent justice and injustice don't even really exist.* For the animals, there's no cry of "Injustice!" when the lion kills the lamb. That's just the way it goes. Animals and their experiences just *are.* And if that's the case, can we attribute to animals any transcendent meaning or value? And if we take life as it simply appears, again without considering any overarching metanarrative *beyond the sun,* do we have any reason to believe that the meaninglessness we see in animal life doesn't apply to human life as well?

The atheist biologist Richard Dawkins describes life this way in a now often-quoted passage. See if you can identify how he resonates with Solomon's "under the sun" observations:

> During the minute that it takes me to compose this sentence, thousands of animals are being eaten alive, many others are running for their lives, whimpering in fear, others are slowly being devoured from within by rasping parasites, thousands of all kinds are dying of starvation, thirst, and disease. . . . In a universe of electrons and selfish genes, blind physical forces and genetic replication, some people are going to get hurt, other people are going to get lucky, and you won't find any rhyme or reason in it, nor any justice. The universe that we observe has precisely the properties we should expect if there is, at bottom, no design, no purpose, no evil, no good, nothing but pitiless indifference.[42]

Dawkins is an atheist, believing that the universe was caused by unknown purposeless forces in the big bang and that life then arose to the complexity we see today through the blind, physics-bound forces of evolution. So there's no God and certainly no overarching story that we're a part of, no divine plan working itself out, no transcendent values like good and evil. Dawkins often points out that he can't prove there's no God and thus no divine plan. But he thinks his observations of the world clearly line up with this belief: "The universe that we observe has precisely the properties we should expect if there is, at bottom, no design, no purpose, no evil, no good, nothing but pitiless indifference."

What are these observations? A universe marked by immense, immeasurable amounts of death. As a biologist, he's well in tune with the amounts of death within the biological world. In fact, atheistic evolution has death as its bedrock and heart: Survival of the fittest is nothing but species fighting tooth and nail to escape premature death and pass their genes on to the next generation. Couple this with random genetic mutation and you have neo-Darwinian evolution. And after making these observations within his study of animal biology, Dawkins finds no trouble in making the same observations in human life: "Some people are going to get hurt, other people are going to get lucky, and you won't find any rhyme or reason in it, nor any justice."

And so the conclusion is obvious: If there's no God and if we see general animal life as really not all that different from human life, there's no difference in value between the two. To the forces of the universe, humans are simply a subset of animals, existing in a universe of "no design, no purpose, . . . nothing but pitiless indifference." In a way, this echoes what Solomon says considering life "under the sun": Our experience is that humans are "like . . . the animals." Just as Dawkins says this is "a universe of electrons and selfish genes," Solomon says this is a universe of dust and injustice.

"Under the sun," we seem to be left completely in the dark with whether or not there is anything more to death than this. Solomon even says, "Who knows if the human spirit rises upward and if the spirit of the animal goes down into the earth?" Remember that he is making the observations of one "under the sun." There are some questions about the original Hebrew wording here, and translators have offered several different meanings. But the general idea is clear: "under the sun," that is, just from empirical observation, we can't know anything about what awaits us after death. (Remember Hamlet's question?) We are left simply with a world marked by the finality of death, and so by the meaninglessness and valuelessness of human life.

Solomon's response, again "under the sun," is rather tepid: "There is nothing better for a person than to enjoy their work, because that is their lot. For who can bring them to see what will happen after them?" In other words, if this is all there is, try to enjoy it as much as possible, because, as Hamlet says, who knows "what dreams may come"? But this is the enjoyment of escapism, of trying to get in as much as possible before the big sleep. This is not a fulfilled life, a life looking hopefully to the future and already seeing on the horizon the triumph of justice and love. ("For who can bring them to see" that?) This is not the truly transcendentally meaningful life people are looking for.

STARDUST

"All come from dust, and to dust all return." But what's so bad about dust? Maybe the dust could be from somewhere really special. In a documentary titled *Planetary*, the Apollo astronaut Edgar Mitchell describes his experience of seeing from space the Earth alongside the moon and sun, with the black veil of infinity behind them:

> **I had studied astronomy, and I had studied cosmology, and fully understood that the molecules in my body and the molecules in my partner's body and in the spacecraft had been prototyped in some ancient generation of stars. In other words, it was pretty obvious from those descriptions we're stardust.**

As Mitchell experienced this radical perspective shift of seeing everything from space, he couldn't help but see himself, his fellow astronauts, and the Earth in a different way. When you talk to your friend, you're not typically thinking about their molecular biology, but rather you see your friend as a *person,* as a self-aware being like yourself. As you go through the daily grind, you experience and view your house in an anthropocentric (or human-centered) way, that is, as *your home.* Your dog is a *companion* (albeit a different kind than your human friends). But all of this faded into the background for Mitchell. It was probably still there in his mind, but instead what Mitchell saw first was that these things—all these things we experience as *person, home, companion*—given an evolutionary big bang cosmology, are all *stardust.* That is, presumably billions of years ago when the stars formed, all the matter that would become *us* also formed, starting with hydrogen and helium atoms being created by the actual big bang, and then the heavier elements formed after a few generations of stars died. And after billions of years, through the forces of physics, we were produced. So regardless of what we *look* like right now, we're essentially, at the root of it, dust from stars.

This observation is *meant,* for the purposes of the documentary, to have the effect on us of driving home the interconnectedness between us and our planet—all sharing the same majestic origin. It's *meant* to make us care more for the planet and the environment.

But it may, unfortunately, have the reverse effect. Think for a moment: if everything is essentially stardust, what implications does this have for their *value?* If a star explodes millions of light years away, and in its explosion destroys a few planets around it, what would it matter to you? What are the odds that you, or anyone on earth, would ever even find out about it? It's essentially a star destroying other things around it made from stardust. It's simply a physical event taking place. It's neither good nor bad. It just *is.* It's just *stardust.* At most, it might be an excuse to find someplace where the glow from the streetlights won't get in the way of trying to see the nova for yourself (and maybe a few shooting stars with it, if you're lucky). All right then, what if our *own* star were to explode? How would it be different, really? It would destroy us and the other planets around us, but is there some objective reason it should matter more? In a million years, some stargazers on another planet will enjoy the show. End of story. From the perspective of the cosmos, if our *own* star, the sun, exploded and destroyed us along with it, all that would change is the location of that explosion. Nothing else. Just as stardust on the other side of the universe is rearranged, so it's rearranged here.

I don't think Mitchell believed that we're nothing *but* stardust, that there's nothing more in way of explanation to describe humanity. He might very well have said that's only the starting point, that there's far more to talk about. But given atheism, if stardust *is* the starting point, if the metanarrative for our universe begins with a natural, albeit timeless, spaceless, "causeless" event (according to the theory, time and space and therefore causation as we know it didn't exist in the first moments of the big bang), then the end point is also stardust. Or maybe mere dust, floating in a vast nowhere, never to be part of a new star or any other being ever again. There's no way to bring into the story transcendent, cosmic value.

Meanwhile we *want* to say so much more. In the 1970s, another Mitchell, the songwriter Joni Mitchell, wrote an anti-war song about traveling to 1969's pivotal outdoor music festival Woodstock. In that song titled after the festival, she wove in some heavy theological themes. She says we are all stardust, but somehow, she pines, we need to see ourselves as more than that. Somehow we "got to get ourselves back to the garden." Mitchell was comparing the Garden of Eden with Woodstock and the values of Woodstock, envisioning free love, pacifism, and good music bringing about a restoration, a return to an idyllic state of perfection, and turning bombers into butterflies (like how the Bible describes swords being turned into plowshares in its visions of an Eden-like heaven).

Joni Mitchell is not alone in her longing. Many today are crying out that we need to somehow see ourselves and all humanity as *more than* dust, as beings of value, beauty, purpose, and transcendent meaning, beings who regardless of skin color or status shouldn't have bombs and napalm dropped onto them or be attacked with dogs and fire hoses. We need to find a *different* metanarrative, perhaps even something like a biblical one that sees us as coming from the hands of a Creator-God who loves us, brought us into being, and desires to be with us, just as Adam and Eve were with God in the garden. According to the biblical metanarrative, Adam, the first human, was made from dust. But he was not *essentially* dust alone. That was only the outward form. He was also a *soul,* that is, a person or ego with an eternal quality to him, because God wanted to spend eternity with Adam. That is how the Bible's Story starts; that is where the Bible says our dust starts—in the garden. But how *do* we get back to the garden?

We'll get there. But we are not done with those who say there never was a garden. Some say the goal is not to get back to a good God and his gift of a garden; rather, the key to the truly good life is liberating oneself once and for all from the notion of any God or garden. True joy comes from dependence on yourself, not a cosmic Gardener. The goal is to rejoice in your cosmic independence and aloneness. What is this joy they claim to have found? Is there joy in being only dust?

SARTRE AND AUGUSTINE, ESSENCE AND EXISTENCE

Different philosophers have struggled with how to cope with the implications of an atheistic understanding of death. If from stardust we come and to stardust we return, how ought this shape the way we live? How can we talk of life and *the choices we make during our lives* as having value? Some believed the proper way forward was to focus on orienting the discussion and oneself toward death. For example, Martin Heidegger (often called an existentialist, although like Camus he rejected the title) believed that the key to finding a meaningful life lay in this orientation toward death, what he called being-towards-death.

Other philosophers, though, notably our French existentialists, believed the finality of death ought to turn our focus away from a death we can't control and more toward *this* life and the things we *can* control. If there's nothing to come, then what we do *now* is of the greatest significance. In fact, it's of the *only* significance, since there's literally *nothing* once one dies. And in the significance of what we do now, the choices we make before we die, perhaps we can talk of value to our lives. The existentialists' most popular philosopher, Jean-Paul Sartre, attempted to find this value by meditating on our ability to make choices. Sartre suggested that humans could define themselves through their choices. He argues:

> What do we mean by saying that existence precedes essence? We mean that man first of all exists, encounters

himself, surges up in the world—and defines himself afterwards. If man as the existentialist sees him is not definable, it is because to begin with he is nothing. He will not be anything until later, and then he will be what he makes of himself. Thus, there is no human nature, because there is no God to have a conception of it. Man simply is. . . . Man is nothing else but that which he makes of himself. . . . [T]o say that we invent values means neither more nor less than this; that there is no sense in life *a priori*. Life is nothing until it is lived; but it is yours to make sense of, and the value of it is nothing else but the sense that you choose.[43]

What was he getting at with those terms, *existence* and *essence*? How could a person exist before he had an essence? These are old concepts. And Sartre was trying to say that Western thinkers had had them backwards for centuries.

Around 1,600 years ago, a Christian thinker named Augustine of Hippo (the present-day city of Annaba, Algeria) said that when it comes to the essence of each human, "The essence that is established as a created thing antecedes in the word of God the creature that is established."[44] That is, the *essence* of a particular human is present *before* that human physically begins to exist in the world. How? She exists in the mind of God first. Think of it this way: A master woodworker sets out to create a chair. Before the wood is fitted together or even cut, the chair already is known somewhere else first: in the mind of the woodworker. The woodworker pictures the chair in his mind or creates blueprints for the chair, and then he brings the chair into physical existence by crafting and carving it out of the wood. The essence of the chair first was in the woodworker's mind, and *then* the woodworker brought the chair into existence. Similarly, the biblical metanarrative says that before the world was created, even before time and space, every human being who would ever exist was fully known in the mind of God. He knew exactly who they would be, what they would become, where they would live, what role they were to play in his *providence*—his work of caring for, protecting, and satisfying all life—and in his Story of unfailing love.

This is also the Teacher's metanarrative, the Story he believes truly runs through everything. Despite the appearance "under the sun," every day of it is "life God has given" (Ecclesiastes 5:18; 8:15; 9:9)—it is good times and bad "God has made" (7:14), first envisioned in the mind of God before they ever came into being. Speaking to you and me, the readers, the Teacher says, "Remember *your* Creator" (12:1, emphasis mine). He knew each one of us as his creation, before he assembled us in our mothers' wombs (11:5). And each person's very soul he personally placed inside of them: "The spirit returns to God who gave it" (12:7). Every individual's essence—every ridge of their fingerprints, every contour of their soul—was *first* fully known by God. *Then* God brought them into existence. Essence precedes existence.

And this is breathtaking! If your essence preceded your existence, if you were first thought up in the mind of a perfectly loving God, then that means you have tremendous value. Think of this for a moment: God *decided* to create *you*. He thought you up and said, "That would be a wonderful person to spend eternity with," and then he brought you into existence. You are his precious creation, far more valuable to him than a masterpiece to its artist. From an ancient Hebrew song: "I am fearfully and wonderfully made" (Psalm 139:14). If God made you, you *are* a masterpiece.

Each person's value as a human being comes directly from the fact that God values them, that he loved their essence enough to bring it into existence. To know that God created you just so he could be with you is truly amazing. As the writer George MacDonald puts it:

> **I would rather be what God chose to make me than the most glorious creature that I could think of; for to have been thought about, born in God's thought, and then made by God, is the dearest, grandest and most precious thing in all thinking.**[45]

It also means that God writes his metanarrative with you in mind. Just as a playwright creates characters *for* the story and the story *for* the characters, you have been brought into being *for* the metanarrative and the metanarrative brought into being *for* you. The whole story of God's salvation of humankind was planned and executed *for you*. Further, God places you exactly where you need to be in life. Even though all the choices we make are absolutely free, God planned the story of our world ahead of time, knowing the choices you would make and working it out all for your good. If essence precedes existence, and if essence has its source in the God described by the Bible, then your life is of infinite value (because you are loved by a God of infinite value) and your life has more purpose that you'll ever be able to imagine (because God created it with a role in his Story of this universe).

But Sartre, who is an atheist, says that since God does not exist, this starting point is reversed. He writes in direct response to Augustine: Since there is no God, then *existence* precedes *essence*. And that is a horrible thought. And Sartre knew it. He called this a great burden, a slavery, a condemnation, an abandonment. He fully embraced the notion that there is no cosmic meaning in life. And so he made it his life goal to find a way for people to see their lives as valuable and purposeful while still believing that there is no cosmic meaning to life, that their existence precedes their essence. Does he think he succeeds, and if so, how?

He states clearly that if a person's essence does not precede their existence, "to begin with he is nothing." In other words, a person starts in this world as a blank slate: no personal identity, no goals, no purpose, certainly no value. He just *is,* an ego that has come into the world—nothing more. But he doesn't stay that way: he begins to make *choices*. As a child, he begins to decide his favorite colors, his role models. As a young boy, he decides to either work hard or not work hard at school. As a young man, he decides his political leanings, his first career, maybe even who he'll marry. And over time, as these choices are made, he begins to shape who he is and to make himself—his *own* essence.

Sartre believes this is your story, the way you have constructed your own essence over time. "But," you might ask, "is it a *good* essence? How can I assess the person I've become? Did I make *good* choices?" This is tricky because, as Sartre writes, there are no values *a priori*. That is, since there's no God to first think up your essence, then there's certainly no God to first think up values, that is, things like what ought to be right or wrong, whether this or that person's life is inherently important, etc. In other words, there's no *transcendent* morality or *transcendent* value of things. These values are all created as we make our way through life. As in Sondheim's play *Into the Woods*, "*You* decide what's right; *you* decide what's good." And so the choices you make in life construct for yourself your own system of values.

Throughout life, then, you make choices. And you react to those choices. And you choose to value some things and not others. Who you are, your essence and values, then, are "nothing else but the sense that you choose." "Man is nothing else but that which he makes of himself."

If we follow Sartre's reasoning, this means no one *else* can decide who or what you are. This is an important aspect of Sartre's philosophy given the climate in which he lived. Some of Sartre's most influential ideas were written down while he was a prisoner of the Nazis in World War II. Also active in the French Resistance and a strong voice against anti-Semitism, Sartre's work was found to be deeply insightful and encouraging to those dehumanized by the war. Imagine your enemy is attempting to label you, to decide what your value is, to degrade you to the status of a lesser human. What Sartre's philosophy gives us is the ability to say, "No, you don't get to decide my essence; only I do through the choices I make." And so, many have found considerable strength in Sartre's approach to human identity.

To be fair to him, we should also note Sartre's teaching that our absolute freedom as individuals makes us responsible for *all* humankind. What you choose—what you pursue, what you make your life project—determines your values. That is what you deem to be "good." But then you would only be fooling yourself if you did not admit that it would also be good for everyone else to possess that same good thing: "In fashioning myself, I fashion humanity."[46]

To some extent, Sartre tried to live up to this high ideal. He was tremendously active in the social movements of his day. He participated in war crime tribunals and spoke up for political prisoners. The newspaper he helped to found, *Modern Times*, consistently denounced torture and repression, despite severe political repercussions. And finding value in our accomplishments that benefit society, as we explored at length in the previous chapter, is a very tempting way to try to make up for an utter lack of cosmic value.

In the end, when it comes to finding meaning, what Sartre gives with one hand, he takes with the other. Toward the end of his life, he gave a lengthy interview, published as "Self-Portrait at Seventy." Here is the final question of the interview:

> *In short, so far life has been good to you?*
>
> On the whole, yes. I don't see what I could reproach it with. It has given me what I wanted and at the same time it has shown that this wasn't much. But what can you do?
>
> (The interview ends in wild laughter brought on by the last statement.)
>
> The laughter must be kept. You should put: "Accompanied by laughter."[47]

For all his sincere and noble talk of being responsible for the whole of humankind, he says there wasn't really much to life. And he finds this wildly hilarious. Many would admire this about Sartre too. There's something carefree about him. . . . Make what essence you can out of your life. Do not let others define you. Do not wait for some god to come and define you. But at the same time, don't take yourself or your life too seriously. "The laughter must be kept."

MY CHOICES, MY VALUE

Is it something to laugh about? To be carefree about?

Sartre says we shape our own essences through the choices we make. But do I *really* want to be simply the sum of the choices I've made? Should I find this thought liberating?

I find it disconcerting, to put it mildly.

What kind of choices do we make in life? Many of us have made terrible choices. In fact, a good deal of the pain and suffering in this world is the result of human choice: from warfare to a good deal of famine, from broken homes to workplaces plagued with sexual misconduct, from religious radicalism to ethical apathy. Even in our own personal lives, would we be comfortable placing in the newspaper headlines all the choices we make in secret when no one is looking, all the things we do behind others' backs or while cutting corners or while conspiring together against whoever's least popular?

Sartre is right. Our choices certainly do tell us something about who we are. And what do they tell us? In his book of Proverbs, Solomon writes, "Who can say, 'I have kept my heart pure; I am clean and without sin'?" (Proverbs 20:9). Who we are begins with the heart, with the thoughts that flow from inside, with the choices of what to think about, what to fantasize about, what to play out in our minds. Whether or not the anger, hatred, or pettiness I think about make themselves evident in a public action, even just harboring those thoughts and emotions inside myself surely tells me something about who I am. This honesty about who we are is part of Solomon's assessment of things in Ecclesiastes:

> Indeed, there is no one on earth who is righteous,
>   no one who does what is right and never sins.

> Do not pay attention to every word people say,
>   or you may hear your servant cursing you—
> for you know in your heart
>   that many times you yourself have cursed others.
> (Ecclesiastes 7:20-22)

Solomon encourages us to be careful about how we judge the actions of other people, because the evil we find in the world around us we also often find within ourselves.

And what if we think we're making the right choice, but we're not? Solomon also wrote in Proverbs, "A person may think their own ways are right, but the LORD weighs the heart" (Proverbs 21:2). We deceive ourselves, we wear away our consciences over the course of a life of bad choices, and we often become ethically jaded because of a society that embraces evil. How many Germans during the Holocaust justified to themselves their own racism and dehumanizing acts because their government publicly embraced those evils in parades and speeches? How many Americans thought nothing of the evils of slavery or of the brutal displacement of Native communities because the society publicly embraced those evils in parades and speeches? What evils today have we become comfortable with because of a society that publicly embraces those evils in parades and speeches? Remember Joni Mitchell calling us to go back to the garden by revolting against the injustice we find in this world? How do we even know what to try to replace that injustice with?

> What is the good of begetting a man until we have settled what is the good of being a man? . , , It is as if a man were asked, "What is the use of a hammer?" and answered, "To make hammers," and when asked, "And of those hammers, what is the use?" answered, "To make more hammers again."[48]

We noted earlier how G. K. Chesterton warned us to be very careful when we talk about progress. He noted that, given a godless universe, it was very difficult to speak of *society* progressing toward some goal, whether scientific, technological, or political. A metanarrative, a plotline for society, is needed if we're going to judge whether things are moving in the right direction.

This desire for progress is often applied not only to politics and society but to the entirety of humanity itself—as *a species* (or at least as individual members of our species) we're working at becoming a better version of ourselves than past versions. Do you think that with the right cocktail of conditioning, counseling, and education it's possible for you to truthfully speak the famous autosuggestion phrase of psychotherapist Émile Coué: "Every day, in every way, I'm getting better and better"?

There's a major problem with this thinking, Chesterton points out. If you don't know what the purpose of being human is, how can you tell whether you've made any progress in the right direction? As we've seen, contemporary atheist theories tell us there is no inherent purpose to being human, since humans just happened, since humans are just another type of thing that's formed from stardust and produced by mindless processes like natural selection. And so if there's no inherent purpose, you decide for yourself or, in Sartre's terminology, you *create your essence* through the choices you make. But Chesterton reminds us, given Sartre's worldview, there's no way of proving whether what you've chosen to be is any better than anyone else's choice. Our consciences might make us feel as if we're moving in the right direction, but without a metanarrative, we cannot explain those feelings.

Like hikers lost in a forest, we often can't tell if we're moving in the right direction, often times circling back to the same spot and finding out that after so much work we're no farther than before. Are we surprised, then, when one of our companions says, "It's pointless; we'll never get out; this is meaningless!" Another of Solomon's Proverbs is, "There is a way that appears to be right, but in the end it leads to death" (14:12). We simply cannot trust our own assessments of ourselves; experience has clearly demonstrated it's far too dangerous. We need someone truly good who transcends the mess of humanity if we're to get a truly objective view of who we are and what our true essence is and how good it is.

And so the problem is that we must agree with Sartre. Our choices *do* tell us something about who we are. But Sartre's phrase, "Man is nothing else but that which he makes of himself," is a truly terrifying thought. What have you made of yourself? And we're not even capable of knowing *all* the evil we choose to commit: we're so lost in the woods of our contexts and cultures. The Bible calls for complete honesty about who we are, about the pervasiveness of evil in our hearts that flows daily into our thoughts and actions. And we're playing right into our weaknesses if we believe we can create something *good* simply out of the choices we make. We might be able to create something our neighbors can live with, something bearable and even enjoyable at times for our children to live with, but we can't believe we'll be able to end the injustice of this world and get back to Joni Mitchell's garden; we're part of the problem! The simple and sobering truth is that there's no way we can get back to the garden on our own. What we need is someone like us, but not like us, who can pick us up and carry us through the woods, who *can carry us* back to the garden.

COULD SOLOMON GET BACK TO THE GARDEN?

Ecclesiastes purports to have been written at a point in Solomon's life when he realized he couldn't undo his mistakes. He couldn't fix it. He had ruled over Israel's golden age and then had poisoned the well. Remember the legacy we outlined in chapter 2? Solomon had literally written the handbook for living a just and good life, and then he turned to a life of idolatry, even worshiping gods demanding child-sacrifice. Solomon had literally written the handbook on romantic exclusivity, and then he gathered around himself hundreds of wives and concubines. In response, God told Solomon that he had forfeited the kingship. He warned him that during the reign of Solomon's son—and from then on for generations—Israel would be torn apart and fought over by warring dynasties.

What was left for Solomon to do? He could write one last scroll. He could plead: *Learn from my mistakes.* He knew Israel's golden age was over and his reign would eventually be romanticized as the ideal past. But he wanted his reign, his fall, his chasing after the wind, to instead be a warning. And God let him do this meaningful thing.

He could have written a work on the meaningfulness of life when viewed *over the sun.* He could have waxed poetic about a future afterlife. He could have painted a clear picture of history heading toward hope. But instead he writes on life "under the sun." Why? Perhaps Solomon felt too guilty to be a spokesperson for the gospel. Perhaps he felt too hypocritical. And so instead of instilling hope, he made his mission instead to show as clearly as possible that under the sun, apart from the biblical God, there *is no hope.* All this flowing from the pen of a man acutely aware of where he *ought to stand* before God, given the life he led. Do not mistake the shadow over this scroll as skepticism. It is the shadow of guilt.

> Follow the ways of your heart
> and whatever your eyes see,
> but know that for all these things
> God will bring you into judgment. . . .
> Fear God and keep his commandments,
> for this is the duty of all mankind.
> For God will bring every deed into judgment,
> including every hidden thing,
> whether it is good or evil. (Ecclesiastes 11:9; 12:13,14)

Solomon brings up a future judgment not only to let us know that the evil out there in the world will be set right. He brings up a future judgment to remind you that *you too* need to be set right, as he was. The evil we find within us needs to be set right. Now that he sees his own life clearly, he bids you to see yours a bit more clearly too. We feel the undertones of his penitence, because he desires that we have the same undertones in our lives.

Yes, your choices have meaning, infinite meaning. Make all of them with an awareness that God sees them. Make all of them with his judgment in view.

CAN WE GET BACK TO THE GARDEN?

This is where we stand so far: Solomon makes a big deal about how death makes life for us humans just as meaningless as the life of animals. Dawkins agrees that this is a good comparison. "Under the sun" there is no *qualitative* difference between humans and animals (there is nothing uniquely or essentially different between humans and animals), only *quantitative* differences (humans have aspects that are simply more or less developed than other animals but are essentially of the same stuff, nothing more). And so just as the universe is rather indifferent to other animal life coming and going, so it's indifferent to human life coming and going. It is indifferent to all life being engulfed in the explosions of stars. It just *is,* free of value and free of cosmic meaning.

Sartre agrees with this assessment. No God means no cosmic meaning. *"But,"* he adds, "we can *choose."* At least while we're alive, we're able to construct for ourselves a meaningful life through those choices. He does not claim that our choices give us *cosmic* meaning, but it's a start. And we agree that we do, to a degree, learn something about ourselves from our choices. But what do we learn? What kinds of essences do we discover? Solomon bids us to be absolutely honest: "There is no one on earth who is righteous" (Ecclesiastes 7:20). If we are *only* our choices, we might be troubled by what we find. In fact, if we're honest, we find we contribute to a good deal of the injustice that Joni Mitchell hopes we can overcome.

Think back now to Chesterton's illustration about the hammers. What if there *was* a way of justifying "what is the good of being a man?" The biblical metanarrative supplies just this. It tells us we were created by a *good* God for *good* reasons. We earlier noted how the biblical metanarrative teaches that humans were created to explore and settle this world of ours, to be scientists, artists, and creators—all as mini versions of the Great Scientist, the Great Artist, the Great Creator: God. And after humanity brought pain and suffering into this world through our own choices, choices that separated us from our Creator-God, he promised to fix this relationship through his own choice of love, giving himself through his sacrificial death on the cross. Now he calls us back to him. And as he calls us back, he calls us into new and exciting ways to be humans, created in a new way through faith. We saw at the end of the last chapter how the apostle Paul, one of the most important writers in the Bible, describes it this way: "We are God's handiwork, created in Christ Jesus to do good works, which God prepared in advance for us to do" (Ephesians 2:10).

In the last chapter, we focused on the *work*. Let's now for a moment focus on the *created* part, what Augustine said: Before you ever came into this world, you already *were*. Right there, in the mind of God. And *then* he created you. You are not the product of blind forces.

When we look at a newborn child and have that deep, in-your-gut, emotions-washing-over-you response, we know that it's not simply because evolutionary processes have conditioned us to do that. We know that the child is actually *worth* that sort of response. It's the proper way to react to human life. In biblical words the Teacher would have been very familiar with, humans are "fearfully and wonderfully made; your [God's] works are wonderful, I know that full well" (Psalm 139:14).

The ancient Greeks carved the human form over and over again. The Renaissance artists did the same, declaring the human body an exquisite work of art. The Christian says, "You're right!" The human body, along with the human mind, is unparalleled in showing the masterful hand of its Creator. I can call you beautiful because you *are* beautiful, not simply because our biology conditions us to respond that way. Whether or not there are any humans around to call you beautiful, you are still beautiful. It's objective, rooted in the reality that you were created by a Master Craftsman, God himself.

But we can go one more step, because that's not the creation Paul is talking about. Yes, you were created by God at your physical birth. And yes, part of you knows (or at least *should* know) there's something beautiful about you. Yet we recognize a deep ugliness within us, flowing from what we've called the sinful nature. There's a part of us corrupted, not functioning as it ought to. In the television show *Dexter*, the title character is a serial killer struggling with what he calls the Dark Passenger within him:

> I just know there's something dark in me, and I hide it. I certainly don't talk about it, but it's there—always, this Dark Passenger. And when he's driving, I feel alive, half sick with the thrill of complete wrongness. I don't fight him, I don't want to. He's all I've got. Nothing else could love me, not even . . . especially not me. Or is that just a lie the Dark Passenger tells me?

Although Dexter is meditating on some very specific urges, it's terrifying how much we can relate to this thought of his, isn't it? How many of us, when we take an honest look within ourselves, find this Dark Passenger, these evil urges—an ugly juxtaposition with our sense that there's something beautiful about human life? If we're a beautiful creation by a master Creator, we also know that something has gone very wrong.

And so Paul, when he writes "we are . . . created," is not speaking about that first creation when each of us is born. He's talking about when you've gone through *another* creation process, a *new* birth. When you find out about God's metanarrative, you are born *again* through that knowledge. A new life within you dethrones that Dark Passenger, a new life that now knows *why* you exist (because God loves you and wants to be with you) and *how* you've been called

YOUR LIFE HAS MEANING

to exist (to mirror the love of Jesus through your life by being his hands and feet). But the point is *you are created*. God chose to make and remake you. The Dark Passenger remains, struggling with the new life within you. But make no mistake: you are not the Dark Passenger; you are the new creation, the new life, the new identity created in Jesus. You are remade.

Your time here on earth, then, becomes a time of grace, a gift given to you, a time for God to find you and remake you, a time for you to be his agent for change before the Story this side of heaven ends. You want to do as much as you can before you die *not* because you fear this is it but because you know this *isn't* it. You want to do as much as you can because the love Jesus has shown you has somehow taken hold of you, and you can't help showing it to others. And you know that the times when you give way to the evil that still remains in you, your Savior is right there with you, telling you, "I forgive you; we're good; now get back to it because there's still work to do."

The bottom line is that the Christian knows she is not stardust. Nor are her neighbors. She knows she does not need to get back to the garden. Its seeds are already in her hand, its fruits in her heart, her life.

In *The Lion, the Witch, and the Wardrobe*, C. S. Lewis created a world in which it is always winter but never Christmas . . . that is, until Aslan, the savior-lion, comes. And with him, the cold hopelessness, darkness, and bitterness of our evil-riddled world begin to thaw, and new life appears. Aslan, of course, is Lewis' analogy for Jesus. Because when Jesus comes to us, the cold of our evil-riddled world begins to thaw: The guilt of our wrong choices, the fear of death, the feeling that we're nothing special in this world—it all begins to melt away. And the grass begins to push its way through the slowly warming dirt, the wildflowers bloom, the air begins to smell earthy and full of life, and suddenly we realize we're standing in a garden. We didn't need to go anywhere. He only needed to come to us.

———————— • ————————

SIX.

EVERYTHING IS
MEANINGFUL

—————•—————

THE HUMAN NEED FOR STORY

Michael Chandler and his associates at the University of British Columbia . . . canvassed Native communities through much of western Canada. What struck them almost immediately was the astounding suicide rate among teenagers—500 to 800 times the national average—infecting many of these communities. But not all of them. Some Native communities reported . . . a low of zero (true for 6 tribal councils) to a high of 633 suicides per 100,000. What could possibly make the difference between places where teens had nothing to live for and those where teens had nothing to die for?

The researchers began talking to the kids. They collected stories. They asked teens to talk about their lives, about their goals, and about their futures. What they found was that young people from the high-suicide communities didn't have stories to tell. They were incapable of talking about their lives in any coherent, organized way. They had no clear sense of their past, their childhood, and the generations preceding them. And their attempts to outline possible futures were empty of form and meaning. Unlike the other children, they could not see their lives as narratives, as stories. Their attempts to answer questions about their life stories were punctuated by long pauses and unfinished sentences. They had nothing but the present, nothing to look forward to, so many of them took their own lives.

The Biology of Desire, Marc Lewis[49]

Imagine waking up one day with severe amnesia—no memories of the past, no idea where you are or who you are. This means you don't have a place to call home; you can't identify friends who can reorient you; you're unable to know even in which direction you ought to take the next step. Dr. Michael Chandler reports that something like this has happened on a much larger scale in certain First Nations communities. Teens are suffering from narrative amnesia: They have "no clear sense of their past, their childhood," and with no understanding of how they fit in the past, their future is "empty of form and meaning," that is, they're unable to know even in which direction to take the next step.

We can talk about the many reasons this narrative amnesia affects particularly First Nations peoples and communities: they are literally a displaced people with no home; for many their histories have been largely forgotten, and education is often dramatically lower than in comparative socio-economic communities. And these statistics have been a call to action for Canadians (and ought to be for Americans as well). Isn't it interesting, though, how this study focuses on the importance of narrative in a person's life? There is no hope for the future and so no way of conceiving things as ending well (except maybe by pure chance). If you have no *story,* you have no *purpose.* And if you don't see yourself as having a *purpose,* then why even go through the purposeless suffering of life?

I am using this study as an analogy. I am *not* saying the reason these suicides are taking place is because these kids aren't reading

Ecclesiastes or aren't Christian. I *am* saying this study (and there are others like it) makes clear that seeing ourselves in a story matters. The researchers have put their finger on the fact that within these communities, no story equals no feelings of purpose for these teenagers. The same holds true when it comes to one's *spiritual* purpose and seeing one's life within a cosmic narrative, an overarching story for this universe, *the* metanarrative.

Ecclesiastes is meant to be just that, a demonstration of the deep need for seeing ourselves within the overarching story of God's plan. If we only view things "under the sun," that is, if we see things independent of God's will and purpose, seeing only the daily grind, a collection of cold facts, the bad choices we make—if that's all we see, the logical conclusion is that there's "nothing but the present, nothing to look forward to," nothing but a life empty of cosmic and transcendent meaning. But if we see our lives *over the sun,* that is, in light of God's metanarrative, everything changes: We know that everything is infused with purpose, whether or not we know what that purpose is. We know that everything has its part to play in the grand story, whether or not we know how. We know everything is meaningful.

How can seeing one's life within a story have this dramatic effect? Because not only how we see ourselves but also how we see the world around us are shaped by the story we see ourselves within. In other words, we can picture the biblical metanarrative as not only a story but also a worldview, that is, a lens for how we interpret the world. It's to this aspect of metanarrative we turn next.

THE OVERVIEW EFFECT AND THE "UNDER/OVER THE SUN" EFFECT

In the previous chapter, I quoted astronaut Edgar Mitchell in an interview filmed for the documentary *Planetary*. The film was an expansion of a short film titled *The Overview Effect*, which was produced in anniversary of the space flights that sent back to Earth the very first images of our planet from space. According to the scholars in the documentary, this marked a new moment in our shared consciousness as humans. We had known for some time that we were a planet floating in space, but it's another thing to actually *see* us floating out there, all of our world unified as one small orb in an infinity of dark. This shift of perspective they labeled as the *overview effect.*

Think of it like this: When you were three or four years old, maybe 99 percent of your experiences were extremely localized: your house, your relatives' house, the library, some select stores, a few playgroups. You *knew* there were other kids and people out there, that there were other places, but you never really experienced them. When you started kindergarten, all of a sudden you were exposed to many more cultures—types of people, again, you maybe *knew* existed but had never experienced. And with this new experience, your view of the world changed. When you traveled outside your own city for the first time, your view of the world changed. You already *knew* there were other cities, but now you *knew it* in a way you didn't before, and it changed you as a person. The same follows for the first time you traveled great distances, became friends with very different people, etc. You might have had head knowledge of all this before experiencing it firsthand, but experiencing it firsthand somehow changes you and how you view the world.

This is what happened to us as a species when we received those first photographs of Earth from space. Our worldview changed, seeing firsthand how interrelated and networked everything was on our planet. The folks that produced *Planetary* see it as their mission to constantly remind us of this. In fact, their Facebook page is subtitled: "Planetary Collective is a creative organization dedicated to Worldview Interruption." They want us to think a certain way, and seeing our planet from more than 200,000 miles away certainly jolts the thinking.

Analogously, Solomon is interested in "worldview interruption." He wants us to see the stark difference of life "under the sun" with life, we might say, *beyond the sun*. The book of Ecclesiastes creates in us, rather than the *overview* effect, what we've been calling the *under/over the sun* effect. From the limited perspective of someone simply taking in the empirical data that we see around us, who can be sure that anything has meaning? There's a longing within us that on some level *knows* life really *is* meaningful, but how that's possible isn't obvious or apparent "under the sun." But when a person takes in the Bible and is exposed to God's metanarrative for the first time, it can literally change *everything*. It's a worldview interruption, because now you truly experience things from a different perspective, seeing how interrelated and networked everything really is in the universe as part of God's overarching story of love and redemption.

A shift takes place: On some level you *knew* human life had transcendent value, but now you really *know* it because you now see human life within the metanarrative of humankind deserting God's love and then being restored to it through God literally giving his own life for his created children.

On some level you *knew* that what we do and learn is important, but now you really *know* it because you see how God has created us with purpose and roles to play in the metanarrative, designing us to explore, to discover, to love, and to help one another.

On some level you *knew* there was more to life than what was obvious under the sun, but now you really *know* it because you know there is a good God working out all things for the good of you, his child.

This is the effect Solomon wanted his final confession to have on his successor, his son, and on the coming generations of the kingdom that his sins were about to sunder. This is the effect God wants his Word (through Solomon) to have on you: he wants you to see how utterly empty this world is of transcendent value, how utterly empty it is of fixed meaning without the God of the Bible, that is, "under the sun." He wants to interrupt your thinking with this emptiness.

And then what? If meaning doesn't come from learning, luxury, lovemaking, or laughter, or from accomplishments or so-called progress, should we give up on finding it?

Rather, we should look for it harder than ever.

God wants you to find transcendent value and fixed meaning *over the sun*, in him. His *Story* gives a new view of the world. It injects value, purpose, hope, and meaning into everything. This is Solomon's answer. His alternative. Something to chase after instead of just the wind. Near the end of Ecclesiastes, we find the three most important words in the whole book, the only way back out of the darkness of meaninglessness: Solomon says, "Remember your Creator" (12:1).

REMEMBER YOUR CREATOR

Solomon tells us, "Remember your Creator," and then he launches into a lyrical tour de force of moments in life when remembering our God and his salvation metanarrative are crucial. Solomon expects his readers to have all of God's divinely revealed knowledge in Scripture at their fingertips to *remember from* and to draw on for their picture of what God is like and how God helps them through all these crucial moments. For example:

> **Remember your Creator**
>   **in the days of your youth,**
> **before the days of trouble come**
>   **and the years approach when you will say,**
> **"I find no pleasure in them." (Ecclesiastes 12:1)**

If the Bible is true, and if the salvation metanarrative is true, this is something we want to learn from as young of an age as possible, and we want to learn it well. Because the Bible says that life *will* get rough and painful. People will hate you and hurt you. There will be times when all feels lost, when there seems to be no chance you'll make it through the darkness. There will be times when you say, "I take no pleasure at all in my life." At that time you *must* remember that you can only see a *part* of the story and then turn to the Bible to be reminded of what God says about himself: "Good and upright is the LORD; therefore he instructs sinners in his ways" (Psalm 25:8).

"Though he brings grief, he will show compassion, so great is his unfailing love. For he does not willingly bring affliction or grief to anyone" (Lamentations 3:32,33). Our God is a *good* God, and he is working out for us a *good* story. And we might not be able to see it, and sometimes it doesn't feel like life is heading toward it, but there is a *good* ending. Solomon bids us to begin *remembering,* that is, learning as much as possible, as early as possible in life, that God is *good.*

> Before the sun and the light
>   and the moon and the stars grow dark,
>   and the clouds return after the rain;
> when the keepers of the house tremble,
>   and the strong men stoop,
> when the grinders cease because they are few,
>   and those looking through the windows grow dim;
> when the doors to the street are closed
>   and the sound of grinding fades;
> when people rise up at the sound of birds,
>   but all their songs grow faint;
> when people are afraid of heights
>   and of dangers in the streets . . . (Ecclesiastes 12:2-5)

Solomon begins in our youth, and he now moves on through life, again touching on the transitory nature of everything. The band Death Cab for Cutie meditates on the coming of death in their haunting song "I Will Follow You Into the Dark," singing, "The time for sleep is now / But it's nothing to cry about / 'Cause we'll hold each other soon in the blackest of rooms." There is a very real darkness, when your sun and moon and stars will go dark permanently. For the writer of that song, there's nothing but infinite blackness waiting, and the only comfort found is that you'll be in that infinite blackness with another person. But of course it's tempting to forget that you won't be conscious, you won't experience anyone else ever again, and you as a person will be permanently gone—"in the realm of the dead, where you are going, there is neither working nor planning nor knowledge nor wisdom" (Ecclesiastes 9:10). In short, your life is simply one thing in this universe that arrived and will depart, one out of a great number of transitory things—like the songs of this world that will grow faint and the workers who will eventually become exhausted and their grinding stop. Is everything transitory? Is there nothing permanent?

Compare that to what one biblical poet writes, "Before the mountains were born or you brought forth the whole world, from everlasting to everlasting you are God" (Psalm 90:2). Things might pass away in this world, but there is *one* thing permanent, unmoving, holding all things together. And Solomon says, at this time in your life, *remember him*. And if there is an eternal God that is *good*, might that God desire to spend eternity *with* someone?

The Bible teaches that that someone is *you*. Jesus once said to his students, and he says to you too, "I no longer call you servants, because a servant does not know his master's business. Instead, I have called you friends. . . . You did not choose me, but I chose you and appointed you so that you might go and bear fruit—fruit that will last" (John 15:15,16). Jesus invites you to believe that he has chosen *you* to be his companion for all eternity. And if he has chosen you for eternity, then despite how transitory everything seems in this world, you know that *you* are not transitory, that you will never enter the blackest of rooms, that the songs of the birds might fade but your own songs will never.

> . . . when the almond tree blossoms
>   and the grasshopper drags itself along
>   and desire no longer is stirred.
> Then people go to their eternal home
>   and mourners go about the streets. (Ecclesiastes 12:5)

Solomon describes the winding down of the harvest seasons, when winter is coming and death along with it, when the insects slow and disappear, when the blossoms bloom only to fade and fall dead off the trees. This is all metaphor, of course, for "when people go to their eternal home," for when your own season of life will come to an end. Why must we *remember our Creator* when we face death? Because without the biblical God, the evil, pain, suffering, and death of this world will win. Unless there's another option, *death will win.*

But there is another option. The Bible teaches that *death will not win.*

"Remember your Creator" who revealed this about himself: "God is love. This is how God showed his love among us: He sent his one and only Son into the world that we might live through him" (1 John 4:8,9). Here is God's greatest display of love: His very heart, his mirror image came into this place of dying so that we might live. "This is love: not that we loved God, but that he loved us and sent his Son as an atoning sacrifice for our sins" (1 John 4:10). All of our shortcomings and flaws and the evil within us—that is not what defines us. God has not abandoned us to our preference for empty self-direction. Instead, he sacrificed his own Son, the Fullness and Light of God, to pay for all our beclouded, empty ways. The climax of God's salvation narrative is when God's divine and beloved Son died for us. The climax of salvation history is God's ultimate act of love for you and me.

If you want to know the metanarrative, to be bowled over by the Story, by the love, look to Jesus. Look to the Creator's eternal voice become flesh, his very glory come to earth. Yes, look to his cross—complete forgiveness there. And also look to everything else about him. But most of all, look to the meaning of life he brings: "I have come that they may have life, and have it to the full" (John 10:10).

And so, when you are ready to go to your eternal home, Solomon bids you to "remember your Creator." Remember that this is not the end. Jesus has turned your own death into a passage, a door. And he waits for you there. The Bible describes a Creator who is eternal, perfect, transcendent, absolutely good, and, most important, love. Through his love he sent his treasured, majestic, and only Son to die for us. He calls us back to him from our fallen state. And now he gives our lives eternal value and the work of our lives eternal value—eternal because it is the value of a soul that has an eternity, either with God or separated from him. The only thing that gives life-lasting (cosmic) meaning is remembering this Creator who gives us eternal value and an eternal future with him through Jesus.

Monika is a young woman whom I pastor and to whom I have spent many years teaching the biblical metanarrative. She's been part of many of my group conversations about the meaning of life. On our church website we have a series of articles written by church members about what their faith means to them. Monika wrote one of these articles, sharing her experiences of leaving home to go away to a new university. She writes:

> I started doubting everything: my decision to have moved away from home, my choice in university, and eventually, I also started to doubt God. I had never up to that point experienced such loneliness and sadness so I didn't understand why he would let this happen. During those four months, I talked to God constantly. I turned to passages, read so many times that once used to only be words, but now all of a sudden had so much more meaning. I started looking at his word in a whole new light, and when the suffering finally eased, I realized that I had never been as close to him as I am now. Once again, I saw his hand at work and I was reminded that there's a bigger and better plan unfolding than ours. "'For I know the plans I have for you'—this is the Lord's declaration—'Plans for your welfare, not for disaster, plans to give you a future and a hope'" (Jeremiah 29:11). And there's a certain sense of relief when I think that no matter what happens in my life, good or bad, it is all part of God's plan.

Jesus, through God's biblical metanarrative, gave Monika peace in the face of her troubles. She realized that her sufferings were not meaningless or purposeless but rather that God was working them into his plan, her story within his Story. Her sufferings had meaning. She was valued by her Creator. And she felt *relieved*. It's this relief we can feel even now in the midst of trials that we turn to next.

THE END OF ALL THINGS

> There, peeping among the cloud-wrack above a dark [tower] high up in the mountains, Sam saw a white star twinkle for a while. The beauty of it smote his heart, as he looked up out of the forsaken land, and hope returned to him. For like a shaft, clear and cold, the thought pierced him that in the end the Shadow was only a small and passing thing: there was light and high beauty for ever beyond its reach.
>
> J. R. R. Tolkien, *The Return of the King*

When we stand within a storm, we often cannot see the edges; it looks as if the lightning and rain go on infinitely in every direction. It looks as if the storm will never end. That is not unlike life "under the sun," although at times it may feel more like life *under the storm clouds*—clouds of darkness cast by our wrong choices, stubborn hearts, and shortsighted eyes. And it seems as if it's never ending, that this is the history of humanity and will be until the race becomes extinct. The Bible is for us that shaft of starlight that pierces through, even if for a moment, reminding us that this world, our experiences, our sufferings and sorrows are but a passing thing. It reminds us that there is a far greater world, a much longer Story that stretches behind and before us. The Story began even before the beginning of time with a good God, and it ends in an eternity with a good God.

How do we know that "the Shadow" is only a passing thing, that God is working through the sufferings and sorrows of this life toward a good ending? A Christian leader (the apostle Paul) once encouraged a group of Bible believers (most of whom he had not even met yet) with this very truth—and notice he starts with the confident words "we know":

> **We know that in all things God works for the good of those who love him, who have been called according to his purpose. For those God foreknew he also predestined to be conformed to the image of his Son, that he might be the firstborn among many brothers and sisters. And those he predestined, he also called; those he called, he also justified; those he justified, he also glorified. (Romans 8:28-30)**

This is the confidence we all want, isn't it? We feel that we could easily be included in "those who love him" if we could only be confident that God were actually at work "in all things" for our good. It is a wonderful Story, if one could be sure of it.

And here we read the metanarrative one more time:

> **Before the creation of the world, before time and space came into existence, you already were there in the mind of God. Foreknown. Predestined.**

His purpose for you: be conformed to the likeness of Jesus. That is, every day walk and talk and think and act like Jesus would, in unstoppable love.

His opinion of you in the meantime (while you often find yourself not as loving as Jesus, much at all): justified. You are declared right by the courts of heaven, for Jesus' sake—already appearing to God as his perfect sons and daughters because two thousand years ago Jesus died for you, opening the path to God your Father for you.

His ending for you: glorified. You will be sharing in Jesus' majesty, shining with his light, rejoicing over his Father's love forever, as perfectly as Jesus does.

Your value first and foremost springs from this: You were in the mind of God in the deep infinite past, and you will *be* with God in heaven into the deep infinite future. Your future is made possible through the events of Jesus' life, death, and resurrection on earth.

But how do we know? How can you be sure this Story is real? Three times that Christian leader uses the word "called." If you're already following Jesus, recall your baptism; on that day through water and God's Word you were *called* into God's family and made a brother or sister of Jesus himself. But we can go back further: You're able to be called a child of God because two thousand years ago Jesus died for you, opening the path to God your Father for you. But we can go back *further:* Before your baptism, before the cross, before the creation of the world, before time and space came into existence, you already were there in the mind of God. God had been waiting a long time to baptize you.

And as you've been reading this book, God has been calling you. In fact, *right now* God is *calling* you. Concerning your sins, griefs, emptinesses, and troubles—all of them—Jesus says, *Give me that weight. I've been waiting a long time for it. Before the world began, even before time and space began, I've been waiting to carry it, to carry you.*

And so you hand it to him: your doubts, your feelings of worthlessness and of being lost and adrift in this world are handed over.

And in exchange he opens your eyes, not your physical eyes but your mind's eye, and you see eternity with him.

ADDENDUM FOR PASTORS:
AS YOUR OWN POETS HAVE SAID

In Acts chapter 17, Luke leaves for us a model of Paul's preaching to a Gentile audience. Interestingly, Paul doesn't quote the Bible (at least not in the bit recorded by Luke). Instead, Paul appeals to the natural knowledge of God and so attempts to move, according to good teaching pedagogy, from the known to the unknown. And in doing this, he quotes the Athenians' own secular, unbelieving poets. You and I know that Paul could use even such poets to teach truths about God, because the natural knowledge of God is accessible to all people and so it's reflected in the great art, literature, and thinking of many cultures throughout all of human history.

The author of Ecclesiastes claims that everything in life, considered apart from the biblical God, is meaningless. If we grant that King Solomon wrote Ecclesiastes at the end of his years, reflecting on a life of sinful attempts to accomplish sinful ends, we find in Ecclesiastes an implicit confession of sin: Solomon had turned his life into a chasing after the wrong things for the wrong reasons, and he was admitting that. Even a life of accomplishments as great as his own, he admitted, is meaningless apart from the God of the Bible. This was God's law working on his heart. Along similar lines, we find God's law working, albeit imperfectly, on the hearts of artists, writers, and philosophers throughout all of human history. Many throughout time have reflected that life is meaningless, and they've experienced this because they were considering life apart from the biblical God (whether or not they knew they were doing this).

This book might have as its theme: *As your own poets have said*. This book has been written especially with non-Christians in mind, or at least nominal or biblically illiterate Christians, and so we have attempted, like Paul in Athens, to move from the known to the unknown with our readers. We have provided numerous examples of secular writers and thinkers that you and I know have God's law written on their hearts, and we have shown how these thinkers support Solomon's claim.

But of course, the natural knowledge of God only takes us so far. Solomon says life is meaningless when not considered within the biblical metanarrative, that is, within God's revealed overarching story of his redemption of humankind. And so our response, once we let secular authors help Solomon put the nails in the coffin of the possibility of a meaningful life, is to resurrect the meaningful life through meditating on this gospel-driven metanarrative. And we know the Holy Spirit can work through sharing the gospel to create faith. Like Paul on Mars Hill, it might take us a while to get to that gospel. We had to explore life without the biblical God thoroughly, and so we felt the weight of that accursed darkness. But this was all so that the light of the gospel can shine all the brighter, so that its dawn is all the more welcomed.

People today need a transcendent good Story that is also *real,* one that doesn't leave them meaningless, hopeless, and dying in their sins. My prayer is that this will aid you in telling that Story.

Endnotes

[1] "Broken Chair" written by Chris Anderson and Thomas Hien. All rights reserved. © 2006.

[2] Ecclesiastes 1:2,3

[3] Sowetan Live, "The Weird, Wild and Interesting Goals People Have on Their Bucket Lists," *Sowetan Live Online*, February 28, 2017. https://www.sowetanlive.co.za/good-life/2017-02-28-the-weird-wild-and-interesting-goals-people-have-on-their-bucket-lists/

[4] Ecclesiastes 1:11

[5] Words and Music by LEE MILLER, KELLEY LOVELACE and BRAD PAISLEY. Copyright © 2017 WARNER-TAMERLANE PUBLISHING CORP., THE COUNTRY AND WESTERN MUSIC, WB MUSIC CORP., NEW HOUSE OF SEA GAYLE MUSIC, OWN MY OWN MUSIC PUBLISHING and CLEARBOX RIGHTS. All Rights on behalf of Itself an OWN MY OWN PUBLISHING Administered by WB MUSIC CORP. All Rights on behalf of Itself and THE COUNTRY AND WESTERN MUSIC Administered by WARNER-TAMERLANE PUBLISHING CORP. All Rights Reserved. Used By Permission of ALFRED MUSIC.

[6] Tim Ferriss, "General Stan McChrystal on Anti-War Americans, Pushing Your Limits, and The Three Military Tests You Should Take," *The Tim Ferriss Show*, podcast audio, posted July 10, 2015. https://tim.blog/2015/07/10/general-stanley-mcchrystal-on-anti-war-americans-pushing-your-limits-and-the-three-military-tests-you-should-take/

[7] Tim Ferriss, "Peter Diamandis on Disrupting the Education System, The Evolution of Healthcare, and Building a Billion-Dollar Business," *The Tim Ferriss Show*, podcast audio, posted July 17, 2015.

[8] James Hibberd, "A Dance With Dragons Interview," *Entertainment Weekly Online*, July 12, 2011. https://ew.com/article/2011/07/12/george-martin-talks-a-dance-with-dragons/

[9] Ecclesiastes 1:2-10

[10] Ecclesiastes 1:11

[11] Friedrich Nietzsche, *The Gay Science* (1882, 1887) para. 125; Walter Kaufmann ed. (Vintage, 1974), 181-182.

[12] Jean-Francois Lyotard, *The Postmodern Condition*, trans. Geoff Bennington and Brian Massumi (University of Minnesota Press, 1984), xxiii–xxv.

[13] Lyotard originally was not critiquing religious metanarratives but instead overarching philosophical interpretive schema, such as reductionism, Marxism, and Enlightenment metanarratives. Today his critique is applied just as much to religious interpretive schema, or what we will call metanarratives.

[14] Alasdair MacIntyre, *After Virtue: A Study in Moral Theory* (University of Notre Dame Press, 2007), 216.

[15] *Pesikta de-Rav Kahana* quoted in Tremper Longman III, *The Book of Ecclesiastes* (Eerdmans Publishing Co., 1998), 27.

[16] Franz Delitzsch, *Commentary on The Song of Songs and Ecclesiastes,* trans. M. G. Easton (Eerdmans, 1968), 182, 184.

[17] Dr. Duane A. Garrett, professor at the Southern Baptist Theological Seminary, quoted in Greg W. Parsons, "Guidelines for Understanding and Proclaiming the Book of Ecclesiastes," *Bibliotheca Sacra*, April-June 2003, 160.

[18] Jeffrey Tayler, "A Book of the Bible Even an Atheist Can Love," *Los Angeles Review of Books*, October 9, 2016. https://blog.lareviewofbooks.org/essays/secular-inspiration-in-ecclesiastes/

[19] Speech found at https://youtu.be/q_za_b6haXQ

[20] Ecclesiastes 1:12-18

[21] David Hume, *A Treatise of Human Nature* (John Noon, 1739-40), 335.

[22] Thomas Nagel, *Mind and Cosmos* (Oxford University Press, 2012), 13.

[23] Ecclesiastes 1:18

[24] Joel Marks, "Ignorance Is Bliss," *Philosophy Now*, 2004. https://philosophynow.org/issues/45/Ignorance_is_Bliss

[25] Ta-Nehisi Coates, *Between the World and Me* (Spiegel & Grau, 2015), 52.

[26] Martin Luther, *Luther's Works,* edited by Jaroslav Pelikan, Hilton C. Oswald, and Helmut T. Lehmann, Vol. 15 (St. Louis: Concordia Publishing House, 1972), 28.

[27] Chris Johnson, *A Better Life: 100 Atheists Speak Out on Joy and Meaning in a World Without God* (Cosmic Teapot, 2014).

[28] *Disputation Against Fortunatus the Manichaean*, quoted in Edward J. Young's *Studies in Genesis One* (Presbyterian and Reformed Publishing Company, 1964), 43.

[29] Isaac Bashevis Singer, "Genesis," *Congregation: Contemporary Writers Read the Jewish Bible*, ed. David Rosenberg (Harcourt Brace Jovanovich, 1989), 5,8.

[30] Timothy Ferriss, *The 4-Hour Workweek: Escape 9-5, Live Anywhere, and Join the New Rich,* electronic edition (Harmony, 2009).

[31] Epicurus, "Letter to Menoeceus," *Letters, Principal Doctrines, and Vatican Sayings,* trans. Russel M. Geer (Library of Liberal Arts, 1964), 129a.

[32] Soren Kierkegaard, "Either/Or," *A Kierkegaard Anthology,* ed. Robert Bretall (Princeton University Press), 34.

[33] Alvin Plantinga, "Two Dozen (or so) Theistic Arguments," *Alvin Plantinga,* ed. Deane-Peter Baker (Cambridge University Press, 2007), 226.

[34] Ta-Nehisi Coates, *Between the World and Me* (Spiegel & Grau, 2015), 81-82.

[35] Albert Camus, *The Outsider*, trans. Joseph Laredo (Penguin Books, 1982), 115-116.

[36] Ibid., 118.

[37] Albert Camus, "The Myth of Sisyphus," ed. Walter Kaufmann, *Existentialism From Dostoevsky to Sartre* (Meridian Books, 1956), 312, 313, 315.

[38] G. K. Chesterton, *Collected Works*, vol. 1 (Ignatius Press, 1986), 53.

[39] C. S. Lewis, *The Weight of Glory* (Harper Collins, 1949, 2001), 34.

[40] Tim Henderson, "Growing Number of People Living Solo Can Pose Challenges," *PEW*, September 11, 2014. https://www.pewtrusts.org/en/research-and-analysis/blogs/stateline/2014/09/11/growing-number-of-people-living-solo-can-pose-challenges

[41] Quora, "Loneliness Might Be a Bigger Health Risk Than Smoking or Obesity." *Forbes. com,* January 18, 2017. https://www.forbes.com/sites/quora/2017/01/18/loneliness-might-be-a-bigger-health-risk-than-smoking-or-obesity/#7ea1006425dl

[42] Richard Dawkins, *River Out of Eden: A Darwinist's View of Life* (Basic Books, 1995), 131-132.

[43] Jean-Paul Sartre, "Existentialism Is a Humanism," trans. Philip Mairet, cd. Walter Kaufmann, *Existentialism From Dostoevsky to Sartre* (Meridian Books, 1956), 290-291, 309.

[44] Saint Augustine, *Literal Commentary on Genesis* II, 8, 17. Quoted in Hannah Arendt, *Love and Saint Augustine* (University of Chicago Press, 1929), 54

[45] George MacDonald, *David Elginbrod,* vol. II (Hurst and Blackett, 1863), 226.

[46] Jean-Paul Sartre, "Existentialism Is a Humanism," 292.

[47] Jean-Paul Sartre, *Life/Situations: Essays Written and Spoken*, trans. Paul Aster and Lydia Davis (Pantheon Books, 1977), 92.

[48] G. K. Chesterton, *Collected Works*, vol. 1 (Ignatius Press, 1986), 52.

[49] Marc Lewis, *The Biology of Desire: Why Addiction Is Not a Disease,* electronic edition (PublicAffairs, 2016).